Small Business Marketing
What It REALLY Is,
What It's Not,
& How to Do It

Insider Secrets To Attracting A Flood of
New Customers, Clients, or Patients
"They" Don't Want You To Know

Ariel Astrologia

DEDICATION

Paul J. Meyer used to give a talk called "Who Motivates The Motivator?" An interesting question. No one ever really stops to think about it.

It's easy to overlook the fact that even the leaders we look up to—e.g. the championship coaches who works the sidelines and motivates the team—can use a little boost every once in a while.

This book is dedicated to *my* motivator.

To Kris Mae – my greatest supporter, my best friend, my love. You believed in me when nobody else did.

As an aside, I've learned very early on that RECOGNITION is the bargain of all currencies. It costs you very little but can lead to very big payoffs.

Les Giblin, who was an instructor for Dale Carnegie, said something I think we should all remember in both our personal and business lives:

"Every single human being goes through every single day feeling deserving of a thank-you or a congratulation that never comes."

CONTENTS

READ THIS FIRST

There's no need to wait until you finish reading the book to start getting results from it.

As a reader of this book, I would like to give you exclusive **FREE GIFTS worth $696.95.**

You don't have to wait to start reinventing and transforming your business. You don't have to wait for the perfect time or the perfect product, or anything. You just have to get going and start taking action. There's no secret.

There is no shortage of ideas. But there is definitely a shortage of action and implementation.

Why wait until you finish the book to start getting results?

The best time to plant a seed was yesterday. The second best is today. So start right now.

That's why I want to give you **3 FREE FAST-ACTION TOOLS** to help you **implement FAST.** All you have to do is register to:

Join the Free 5-Day "Magnetic Marketing: From Annoying Pest to Welcome Guest" Challenge.

This online event is also FREE and when you *join using my special link*, I'll give you these 3 valuable money-making tools as bonus gifts:

1. **Bonus Gift #1: The "Automatic Appointments" System & Toolkit *($397.00 Value)***

2. **Bonus Gift #2: Ultimate Small Business Marketing Plan Template *($49.95 Value)***

3. **Bonus Gift #3: Hands-On Personal Assistance with Your "2nd Opinion" Ad Critique *($250.00 Value)***

Here's How To Claim Your Free Gifts Today

To take advantage of this offer and get instant access to these money-making resources, simply visit:

www.ArielAstro.co.uk/Gift

Once you're registered, take a screenshot or photo of the "Thank You" page and email it back to Kris at Kris@ArielAstro.co.uk and she'll send you my amazing bonus gifts for free. That's it. Takes less than 2 minutes.

Please note that this offer IS subject to change without notice.

I urge you to act on this opportunity today, right now, while it is fresh in your mind.

About The Structure of This Book

<u>Section One:</u> Talks about why most people fail long before they even take the first step. It rarely has anything to do with what's happening inside their business or their personal lives.

It mostly has to do with what's going on in the back of their minds—their subconscious. The imagined worries and stories they tell themselves that sabotage their chances of winning before they even get a chance to play.

Both success and failure have a lot to do with what's going on in people's heads. I'm talking about their values, attitudes and beliefs. Specifically their self-limiting beliefs.

Most people sabotage themselves before anything ever happens. They talk themselves out of things they wish to do. They find all sorts of excuses that justify not taking action.

Without a solid Belief-System about yourself and the business you're in, even if you start, you'll never really go far. Somewhere down the road, you'll find a perceived problem and use that as an excuse to not take action or to simply fold over and cry.

Section One is all about breaking these chains of self-limiting beliefs that's holding most business owners and entrepreneurs back from pursuing their ideal business life and from reaching their full earning potential.

Most problems in business aren't really business problems. They are PEOPLE problems. Most businesspeople just can't get out of their own way.

The majority of Section One will dive into Why People Fail and I'll give you a set of proven Governing Principles to rewire your brain and get rid of the societal head trash that you've been conditioned to believe growing up.

When I say this, a lot of people nod in agreement. But I know they don't really "get it" because their behaviour is still the same as the Mediocre Majority. We MUST fix the person first before we attempt to fix any business-related stuff.

Section Two: I'll share with you the entire step-by-step, proven strategy and system for creating effective marketing campaigns. I'll reveal an entirely different, radical, and controversial way of thinking when it comes to your marketing and advertising.

If you're a new business owner or you've only been in business for a few years, I'll show you how to stand out from the crowd, get noticed by your ideal prospects, run circles around your competition and beat the "big dogs" in your competitive area.

If you're an already established business, you'll still benefit from this book as I'll reveal even more profit-generating ideas and strategies to maximise the effectiveness of what you're already doing. You're very likely to find "hidden opportunities" you're missing out on only because you're too close to your business and can't look at it with fresh eyes.

CAUTION: When you "get it"—when you implement and start getting vastly superior results compared to the rest of your industry peers, you'll be judged and criticised for it. What you're about to learn is *that* different.

It's counterintuitive to how most people do marketing—which is why most marketing fails and why ultimately most marketing agencies fail to deliver what they promised.

As an aside, ask any marketing agency to explain in detail the step-by-step system they follow to market, advertise and promote their own business and services. Most will look at you like a deer in headlights. They don't know.

Most of these guys don't even do any marketing and advertising to acquire new clients for themselves. Most of them rely on the hope that their current clients will refer them to a new one.

Relying on referrals and word-of-mouth isn't necessarily bad, but for the most part, it only works for already established businesses who started when there was very little competition in the marketplace.

Most marketing and advertising agencies are doing random and erratic acts of attempted marketing. They don't understand. They don't actually have a "new client acquisition system".

You'd expect a marketing agency to know how to market their own businesses. Yet most don't. I'll share with you why and what you can do to avoid being taken for a fool and making costly marketing decisions.

INTRODUCTION

"If I have seen further than others, it is by standing upon the shoulders of giants." – ISAAC NEWTON

Congratulations. You made a great decision to grab a copy of this book, and an even better decision to crack it open. You are smarter than the average bear.

First, I want to point out a very interesting fact about people who go into business for themselves. The fact that most business owners don't fully understand the REAL business they're in. They mistakenly believe that simply by being "good" at what they do entitles them to more customers, more money, more rewards.

Wrong. Having a "good" product or service is simply the ante to play the game. Everybody has to have one to offer to the marketplace. It is not, however, the thing that separates you, differentiates you, or entitles you to more and better customers.

The REAL business you are in is the Marketing Business.

The business of generating leads, appointments, sales; acquiring customers, clients, patients, members, donors etc.

Why? Because that's where the MONEY is. Without money, capital, funds, moolah—there is no business. A small business with no capital, no cash flow, no money, is (or soon to be) a dead business. It's very agonising, naive and frankly foolish to try and succeed without money.

It pains me to see how many small businesses set up shop, all excited about their new venture, only to shut their doors in less than 12 months—and all they're left with are debt, money worries, and family aggravation keeping them up at night.

The fact of the matter is, effective marketing is a major Achilles heel for most small businesses. The overwhelming pressure to stand out, get noticed, turn strangers into leads, leads into appointments, and converting these leads or appointments into first-time buyers is a colossal challenge for just about any small business owner.

Not to mention the slew of so-called experts giving you all sorts of conflicting advice about how to run and grow your business. I'll let you in on a little secret: most experts today are WRONG. You'll discover why as you read on. It'll be so obvious to you once you "get it."

So in this book, I'm going to talk about a radically different and PROVEN system for attracting your ideal prospects to your business and have them coming to you already pre-interested and predetermined to do business with you versus any and every other option available to them.

If you're like most small business owners, you've probably tried many marketing & advertising ideas before, only to produce little to no results. Or worse, even losing money without knowing why.

I am here to mute ALL the noise. To guide you to the truth and clarity about what really works when it comes to acquiring customers and growing your business in today's ruthlessly competitive marketplace and economy.

Why You Should Listen To Me... And Where These Ideas Originated

My name is Ariel Astrologia. I am the Founder and Direct Response Marketing Strategist of Beat The Control (my copywriting/consulting practice).

I am the author of another book *7 Biggest Advertising Mistakes Small Business Owners Make, And How To Avoid Making Them*", which focuses specifically on the biggest and costliest advertising mistakes, advertising strategy and how-to information.

I am also the creator of *The Automatic Appointments Toolkit*™—a transformational marketing system complete with "done-for-you" and "fill-in-the-blanks" marketing & advertising tools, resources, and templates.

Now, a quick backstory.

When I first ventured off on my own as a marketing consultant, I was only 23 years old. I was living in my parents' house and I've just quit my job at a relatively well-known marketing company.

Why? Well, because I discovered that most people in the marketing industry don't even know how to market themselves. I was very confused, disappointed and felt very angry because I was making money for people who didn't know a thing about marketing and advertising.

So I decided to venture out on my own and declare myself a marketing consultant. And even though my father tried his best to dissuade me (because he was well aware of the high failure rate of people who start a business), it just turns out that:

1. I love helping other small business owners, and…

2. Like most business owners and entrepreneurs, I was absolutely unemployable. I knew the risks and I decided to continue regardless.

At first, I really struggled. Because it was VERY hard to find clients… clients that had a serious ambition to grow… and clients willing to pay me my desired level of compensation.

I soon realised that I can be the most ethical, hardest-working, most knowledgeable and skillful marketing consultant and service provider in the marketplace, but if I don't have enough paying clients, I'm going to starve to death.

I then made another mistake that I bet you also made. I looked around at what all my peers and competitors were doing—the other consultants and marketing service providers—and I copied them (only striving to do a little bit better). I did things like:

- Building a website

- Doing SEO and other Google-related stuff

- Posting non-stop on a number of social media channels (exhausting!)

- Spamming groups and forums trying to sell my stuff

- Burning money doing paid ads without having a clear plan or strategy (e.g. Facebook Ads & Google Ads)

- Sending direct mail letters and postcards… and cold emails!

- Even cold calling and knocking on doors…

In other words, I was doing RANDOM and ERRATIC acts of marketing and advertising. Wasting a ton of my own time and money. Facing constant rejection and humiliation.

In my first few years, I was putting in my share of 16-hour days working 7 days a week. A terrible way to live. By the end of the first year, I was a dismal failure.

My dad was right. Starting, owning and running your own business is hard. I almost made the decision to pack it all up and quit. But the problem I had was I had nowhere else to go. My attitude meant I was practically unemployable. I dreaded the thought of getting a job.

So I was forced to figure out how to make this thing work. So I kept going and I tried everything. I invested in myself and studied absolutely everything about business-building that I can afford and get my hands on. I was hungry… both literally and figuratively. I had to figure this out, or I don't eat.

Turns out, hunger is a great motivation.

My life only began to change when I finally learned that being "great" at what I do doesn't matter if I had no willing, able, and ready buyers to present "great" to. Here's the giant revelation that completely turned my life around:

Without a steady stream of people with whom I can exchange value for money with, NOTHING else about my business matters.

Combine this realisation with a great product or service, and you're unstoppable.

Unfortunately, most business owners only have their product/service, but they never figure out a consistent, reliable, and predictable system that feeds them new leads and buyers every day.

Please stop to appreciate the previous few paragraphs. I blew through a couple fortunes before I figured it out.

Today, I pick and choose who I want to do business with. I'm no longer forced to accept a problematic client just to keep the lights on. I no longer deal with the pain and frustration of begging, hunting, and chasing "would be" clients, who in fact will "never be."

Instead, I attract my ideal customers and clients who come to me already predetermined to do business with me. I'm seen as a trusted advisor rather than "just another salesman" or replaceable vendor.

And unlike many of the so-called experts and consultants nowadays, I eat my own dog food. Aside from my copywriting & consulting practice, I also create, market, and sell my own products and offers to my clients/customers.

In fact, one of my recent ad campaigns—in a market where I had ZERO reputation in—had 43 of my ideal prospects coming to me, wanting to do business with me (most bought products, a handful bought consulting)... Plus 102 good quality leads that can still be further developed and monetized.

I had to stop the campaign early because I didn't need any more work from it (always a good problem to have). I choose to only work with a handful of clients at any given time. I don't want many, and I don't need many in order to live the lifestyle I want to live.

I want you to know that I'm not saying any of this to brag. Only to demonstrate to you that I am a practitioner of what I teach. I try to be my own lab rat as much as possible and I do spend my own money doing the things that we're going to talk about in this book.

The very same methods that attracted you to me are based on the real-world strategies and techniques I'm going to reveal in this book.

Now that you know a little bit more about me, here's a little disclaimer because I want to give credit where credit is due.

I wish I could tell you all the ideas in this book were the results of my own breakthrough inventions. I wish I could just force you to see me as some kind of marketing and advertising genius.

The truth is, I'm not. I rarely invent anything, and when I do, it's rarely worth writing about. What I am is an immigrant boy from a poor, working class family. I came into this country (UK) without knowing a word of English.

After realising I didn't have any special skills or academic ability, I figured that getting into business, marketing, advertising, and sales were my only ticket to being able to live a comfortable life and provide for my family.

In other words, I bumbled my way into business. I got into this game with no previous knowledge, background, or rich relatives to fall back on.

What I do possess is the burning desire and genuine ambition to get rich and stay rich. A desire instilled in me as a child. Bred from real-life experiences of poverty, and of "what I heard at the top of the stairs." Adult conversions about money and our lack thereof.

This led me down the path of becoming a collector of big, elegant business ideas and solutions. I embarked on a harsh and often lonely journey seeking ideas that'll not only multiply my income, but also to build my wealth for generations to come.

And because of that curiosity, I have discovered and formulated a shortlist of little-known, "underground" business-building ideas and strategies that are ACTIONABLE and EVERGREEN.

In other words, they have been proven to work time and time again, in many categories of business, regardless of economic pressure and uncertainty.

In this book, I have organised them for you with the sole purpose of helping you grow your business and get more of your best customers, clients or patients to come to you, already predetermined to do business with you.

You will no longer have to suffer "bad leads" ever again—the time wasters, the tire kickers, the looky-loos. When you finally grasp and take action on the ideas, concepts and strategies within this book, you would only be dealing with high-probability prospects who are already pre-conditioned to accept your proposition and are eager to move forward with you.

You may have seen or heard of these ideas and strategies before. That's because they have already proven to work for hundreds of businesses in many different industries. But with all the noise and clutter in the business world today, chances are, you haven't. At least not in the way that I'm about to reveal to you.

With this book, I am sharing with you the power to see further than the rest of your peers and competitors, because now, you are standing on the shoulders of these giants with me.

Some of these giants are no longer with us. And while others have been mentors to me, it's important to realise that their clocks are also ticking.

I am incredibly grateful for having been given the gift of **authentic ambition**, which led me to the discovery of my mentors. That's why I feel a strong sense of duty and obligation to share their message with you, and to as many business owners and entrepreneurs as I can.

This is my way of saying "thanks" to them because without their hard work, you wouldn't be here reading this gem of a book that has the power to transform and reinvent your entire business life.

If you didn't make the wise choice of getting your hands on this book, you would instead still be lost in the bloody red ocean of "me too" competitors, all starving, fighting for scraps, wasting time on the lowest quality, penny-pinching prey.

That said, in no particular order, I would like to thank and acknowledge my mentors… the true geniuses behind this book. They deserve every credit. I suggest you buy and study everything they have for sale:

Dan Kennedy, Russell Brunson, Bill Glazer, Lee Milteer, Gary Halbert (and his sons Bond & Kevin), Jay Abraham, John Carlton, Darcy Juarez, Ryan Deiss, Drayton Bird, Brian Kurtz, Craig Simpson, Ben Settle, Ken McCarthy, Michael Masterson, Adam Witty, Eugene Schwartz, Clayton Makepeace, Claude Hopkins, Victor Schwab, Rosser Reeves, David Ogilvy, Joe Sugarman, John Caples, Napoleon Hill, Jim Rohn, and last but certainly not the least, Earl Nightingale.

Most so-called experts don't give credit to who they learned and copied from. I do. I have no fear in admitting that I have never invented anything in my life. Here are three reasons why:

1. There is NOTHING new under the sun.

2. True experts are STUDENTS, not masters.

3. True experts GIVE CREDIT to their sources of knowledge, skill, and success.

Somebody learned from somebody who learned from somebody. That's how this works. This is the truth about "experts." None of these people today invented anything new. Maybe new language and buzzwords, yes. But nothing new that is meaningful and profound.

Unfortunately most so-called experts think it'll mess up their image if they give credit to the people they learned from. Most claim they've invented something "new." Lies.

Personally I don't want to endure the suffering pioneers had to endure. So I don't invent. I only take what's working and model/apply it to my current situation.

However, I do believe it's important that I let you know the truth that I am not the only expert in this field who knows what they're talking about. I've learned from many.

You need to be aware of who I learned from so you, yourself, can enrich your knowledge and learn from many different sources—without my help.

The value of a book like this comes from painstakingly finding the information, applying ideas, identifying what works and what doesn't, organising the most powerful ideas and strategies, and teaching it in an easy-to-understand way—NOT from having "new" information. Realise that **peddlers of "new" information often do so because it's easier to sell than the tried and true.**

There are a lot of charlatans in my field teaching marketing who don't really care whether you get smarter, or whether you obtain any results.

What they care about is trying to convince you to buy their high-priced courses or coaching or whatever expensive package they're peddling at the moment.

I've decided from the very beginning not to be one of them.

Now that you know a little bit more about my story, how I came to be, why I'm here, and where these ideas originated from, let's get right into the book.

The next two chapters of this book are the most important because without understanding and overcoming these mental blocks, you're bound to fail no matter what.

So don't skip them. Read on.

SECTION ONE

WHY PEOPLE FAIL

Chapter 1: Why People Fail

I'm going to preface this chapter by admitting the fact that I don't really like people. I'm a bit of a "lone wolf"... a recluse... a hermit. I prefer the company of books—where I can have candid and meaningful conversations with the minority who are either living or have lived fulfilling lives.

I believe the overwhelming majority of people in the world are wasting their potential. Their imaginations are very limited. Their minds, very narrow and slim. Their interests, very superficial, shallow, surface-level. Their knowledge, not much. Their skills, not much either.

There are a TON, and I mean a TON of reasons why people fail. Most of the time, people fail because of what's inside their heads, nothing else. What they think about or don't think about has more to do with their constant failure, unhappiness and lack of success than any other factor.

Most people are so crippled by unhealthy thoughts of "What if this doesn't work out"—they end up not doing anything at all. And what happens when you do nothing? Nothing. You stay the same, which isn't necessarily bad.

But if you're a "small time" business owner and you have aspirations of being more than you are, doing something greater, a desire to transform your life, then you've going to have to take risks and take action on ideas that could propel you forward.

In this chapter, I'm only going to point out the **Three "Big Evils"** that guarantees failure BEFORE anything ever happens. And pretty much every other reason can be put within these three categories. Then, we're going to talk about the three BEST ways to conquer these evils.

This chapter is probably The most important chapter in this book. No kind of great marketing or advertising or selling is going to save a business with a crappy owner. Most business problems are not business problems. They are personal problems that leak out and poison everything else around them, including business.

Together we'll break down these mental blocks and get rid of them for good. Later, I'll introduce you to **My Three Governing Principles** which most successful and influential people share. Once you've gotten your major false and self-limiting beliefs out of the way, you're going to open yourself up for greater wealth, prosperity and opportunity.

Big Evil #1: The Fear Of Making Mistakes

I've personally suffered from this for the longest time. I wanted everything to be perfect, to be of the highest quality, to be the best product or service it can be from its very conception.

Truth is, **almost everything many of us do for the very first time is going to suck.** We're bound to make mistakes, and we're probably going to make a complete fool of ourselves.

But you see, most of the stuff I was so worried about not being perfect, **never happened.** Why? Because I never got round to ever taking action on these ideas. I was too crippled and paralyzed. I couldn't force myself to lift a finger and do something.

Most people don't realise it, but being a perfectionist causes procrastination. We tend to get overwhelmed with worst-case possibilities and scenarios that could go wrong. It causes us to put off doing what we know needs to be done.

The root of procrastination is fear that we won't do something perfect, that we'll be judged. So we're reluctant to even get started. Striving to be perfect creates unrealistic expectations, pressures and problems. It all stems from the self-limiting beliefs and stories you tell yourself in your head.

Typically what would happen is when you were a child, someone made you feel inadequate. This could be a parent, a family member, a teacher, maybe other kids.

From that experience, you formed a belief that it's not okay to make mistakes, and if you do, you'll be judged, humiliated and made to feel terrible.

Reality is, nothing is perfect in this world. No perfect life. No perfect career. No perfect marriage. Regardless of how "perfect" other people try to portray themselves to be, you must come to realise that you're only seeing the very surface level of things.

You're only seeing what they want you to see. It's only logical, since nobody wants others to see how much they actually suck.

So why do we expect ourselves to be perfect? It holds us back from really living. Here's a suggestion: How about **giving yourself permission** to turn your back on that old, self-sabotaging thinking and behaviour?

As of today, do not think of yourself as being a perfectionist who has to get everything right every time. Instead, **think of yourself as someone who is Flexible—someone who tackles problems with an open mind, and is willing and ready to "course correct" along the way.**

Commit yourself to doing just the best you can do, and make corrective changes as you gain more insight, data, and feedback from the marketplace.

Now don't get me wrong. DO commit to a carefully thought-out plan and strategy. However, once you've laid out your plan of action, you must NOT be so rigid that you either completely give up or continue to follow it even if it no longer makes sense.

That's why it's important to do what best you can do with what you have. Then once you're starting to get more and more insight (as a result of taking action and gathering marketplace data), you should make changes to optimise your plan or strategy.

You are not a tree. You're allowed to move and make informed and critical decisions however you see fit.

Please remember that **just as you're able to MAKE mistakes, you're also able to BREAK mistakes.** Continuous improvement is a much more productive and healthier way of thinking than instant perfection.

Michael Jordan once said "You miss 100% of the shots you don't take." It may sound cheesy, but it's true. If you stop and reflect for a few minutes, ask yourself if you can honestly conclude that you're 70-80% ready to do whatever it is you need to do to succeed. If the answer is yes, then you should go and take action.

Another expert in this area, Lee Milteer, once said: "A perfectionist is a person who is always looking for something wrong, finds it (since that's where their focus is) and is then shocked and angry about it. To a perfectionist, any flaw means total failure. This kind of thinking leaves no middle ground and is terrifying—since you're either perfect, or nothing."

Don't wait. You don't need to wait for someone to certify you, or to give you permission to go ahead and do what you want to do. Just go do it.

As long as you believe that it brings value to the marketplace, it's legal, and you're 70-80% ready—do it. You can make corrections along the way. But you'll never go anywhere if you don't start taking action right now. Go.

As a side note: this chapter, itself, is raw and unedited. It's not perfect. It doesn't have to be. I can further add, improve and elaborate on this subject in other content I publish. We keep it moving.

Big Evil #2: The Fear That You Might Actually Fail

Again, whenever you start to do anything new for the first time in your life, chances are, you'll completely suck at it, and you'll probably fail.

That's life. Newborn babies don't come out of the womb and start walking and talking. But overtime, they try and try again. They continue to persevere until they're ready to crawl.

And they continue to crawl until they can balance themselves to stand… until they're able to walk, then run. This cycle is the same for almost everything we pursue in life.

There are very, VERY few in the history of the world who were born with exceptional knowledge, skill or talent. Most successful people are actually very ordinary.

They bumble their way to success. The only difference is they just persisted more, got smarter along the way, continue to make mistakes, continue to learn and therefore continue to evolve.

Ask or study any successful business owner or entrepreneur about the gruesome truth about how long it took them to get to where they are today. Find out how many "failures" they had to face, how many humiliations they've had to endure.

You must learn to accept that what you consider as "failure" is part of life. The real breakthrough here is to NOT think of failure as failure. Reprogram your thinking to **start looking at each and every form of adversity as an OPPORTUNITY masked as adversity.**

In his best-selling book *Think And Grow Rich*, one of the greatest things Napoleon Hill instilled in my mind was the perspective that ***"Every adversity, every failure, every heartache carries with it the seed of an equal or greater benefit."***

This is the mindset you must adopt and practise in order to be successful in business, and most importantly, to be happy in life. You must actively look for the opportunity and benefit hiding behind every problem or challenge you encounter.

Taking risks, making mistakes, the possibility of failure, and the fact that we will inevitably be shunned, judged and criticised by others are all part of the deal. It comes with the decision we made when we decided to become a business owner or entrepreneur.

Because the other side of this is simply to quit and get a job. You choose your struggle here. For me personally, getting a job is too painful. Keeping a job is an impossibility.

My nature and personality just don't fit in with the nature of a J.O.B. There's nothing wrong with it. It's just me. I would rather have a root canal without anaesthesia than get a job.

Anyway, to summarise, internalise this message from Napoleon Hill. I think it encapsulates the whole idea of "failure" – and kills it. Read it again and again and again until it sticks.

Heck, write it down, pen to paper. Many studies have shown you learn better that way. It slows down everything and helps the brain crystallise what you're learning.

"Failure is not a disgrace if you have sincerely done your best.

We live in a competitive world that measures success by winners and losers, and insists that every victory creates a loss of equal dimension.

If one person wins, it seems logical that someone else must lose. In reality, the only competition that matters is the one in which you compete with yourself.

When your standard of performance is based upon being the best you can be - for yourself - you will never lose. You will only improve. Make it a practice to objectively review your performance from time to time.

When you fall short, assess the situation and ask yourself:

Is there anything I would or could have done to change the outcome?

If the answer is no, if you are satisfied that you've done your best, don't waste time reliving the past. Simply learn what you can from the experience, and then get into action again.

If you consistently do your best, your temporary failures will take care of themselves.

Fail forward and reach success faster."

Big Evil #3: The Fear That You Might Actually Succeed

This fear is a bit more discreet. Most people think they are afraid of failure, when in fact, they are afraid of success—the uncertainty of success and perceived problems it may bring into their lives.

There are many reasons why you might feel anxious, worried, or even fear the possibility of gaining success.

From my experience, one of the biggest reasons why people are crippled by the fear of success is because **they feel an immense sense of GUILT** for earning more and achieving more than their family, friends, peers and relatives.

The chief reason most people never attract success, money and wealth is the tremendous amount of guilt burdening their conscious and subconscious minds. The feeling of guilt stems from how they see themselves, their sense of self-worth.

They feel like they don't deserve success, money and wealth—that they're not worthy of all the fine things in life while others are suffering. But here's what you have to understand:

Successful people don't get what they (inherently) deserve. Their success is the result of their **DELIBERATE INTENT** to engineer a process which attracts money, prosperity, wealth, success and abundance in their lives.

Unfortunately most people are not willing to take the risks and go through the pain of success. They'd rather go through the pain of poverty and mediocrity. It's the simpler, more comfortable, more familiar path.

A lot of people fear success because they believe it'll create all sorts of problems for them. Quite true. Having success <u>will</u> create all sorts of problems for you, and most you're going to be unfamiliar with. And initially, you're probably not equipped to handle them.

Here's the flipside: **having NO success also creates a lot of problems.** Settling for what's familiar and comfortable at the moment (i.e. for mediocrity) also creates all sorts of strife, arguments and aggravation in the family.

Which set of problems would you rather have?

Others worry that having success will alienate them from

their friends and family. Here's the honest truth about that: It sure will.

There will be friends whom you grew up with and some family members who just won't "get it" no matter how you try to get them on board, no matter how much you try to help them prosper.

They just won't get it. They're not cut from the same cloth as you and I are. There's nothing we can do about them. It's human nature.

No point in trying to prove human nature wrong. Believe me, I've tried. Many others smarter than us have also tried and we've all ended up disappointed.

The most productive thing you can do for yourself (especially for your health and peace of mind) is to LEAVE THEM BE. Don't try to change them. It's futile.

You can still remain friends and socialise with them from time to time. But honestly, the conversation won't be the same. The stuff you care about are not the same as the stuff they care about.

Most people have too much time on their hands. They concern themselves with trivial knowledge such as celebrity news and "who won the game on Sunday", what they did on their last holiday/vacation, and posting their entire life stories, events and problems on social media.

You and I both know we don't care about that stuff.

We care about progress; about helping people; about increasing our value to the world; making money; building wealth; being a great father, mother, leader; raising great kids with healthy belief systems; and ultimately, living a fulfilling and meaningful life.

Those are just some of the things we care about—the stuff we value. The harsh reality we must learn to accept is that most people don't care about these things, and vice versa—we don't care about their trivialities either.

There's a reason why rich people live in <u>gated</u> communities. It has much less to do with safety and security than the desire to separate themselves from the Mediocre Majority who delves into the trivial, unmeaningful things in life.

Associating yourself with the Mediocre Majority is poison for your thinking and belief system. **You'll only be successful to the point where your belief system takes you.** And most people have very poor belief systems—often not in line with reality, but their perception of reality.

What I'm suggesting is you've got to learn to accept that the pursuit of success—and as a result the attraction of wealth—means that you're sometimes going to just leave some people behind. If they choose to be mediocre, then accept it because it's *their* choice. It doesn't have one damn thing to do with you.

You're going to feel alienated and alone. That's fine. Find yourself other like-minded folks with the same interests and values as you. There are plenty of us out there. We're just a little harder to find, but there are plenty.

Think about it. The mediocre majority in your life—whether they be friends, family, relatives or peers—are not the ones responsible for putting food in your children's mouths. They won't be paying your monthly bills, your mortgage, your phone, your car. They won't fund the lifestyle and autonomy you've always wanted.

Choose Your Struggle Wisely: To Succeed Or Not To Succeed. There Is No "Try."

Now, let's go over how we can overcome and conquer these fears and self-limiting beliefs, and get rid of them forever. When you do this, you'll finally be able to open the floodgates to greater success, wealth and freedom.

In the next chapter, we'll be talking about my three most important **Governing Principles** that you must instil, internalise and reinforce—so that you may enrich your personal life and transform your business life forever.

Both go hand in hand. You must first conquer the things that hold you back in your personal life before you can ever achieve a great business lifestyle.

Chapter 2: Always Start With The Principles

The overwhelming majority of people, including most business owners, move through life without really knowing WHY they're doing what they're doing.

They kind of just move around and let all sorts of things control their lives, their decisions and their movements without really knowing or having a purpose.

One of the most important things you must remember as someone aspiring for a better business and personal life is you must always move with a purpose.

All your actions and decisions must be based on a set of Governing Principles that you strictly adhere to. These principles will pretty much guide how you live your life, what boundaries you set, and conduct business in whichever way you want to conduct business.

Most people do the opposite. They live their lives and conduct business based on what others say and do—friends, family, relatives, business peers, competitors, industry associations etc.

And because most people let others control their lives, they ultimately wind up failing in all sorts of ways: being unhappy, feeling unfulfilled, starting to hate their business, falling in debt, feeling trapped, discouraged and hopeless. Like there's no way out.

You don't have to follow their blueprint. **You can <u>decide</u>** from today onwards that you will control your life, your business, your autonomy. You're not a tree. You're not bound by anything or anyone's opinion of "how things should be done around here."

As long as you don't engage in criminal activities, as far as I and most successful people are concerned, you can <u>make up your own rules</u>, principles and philosophies in life and in business.

I suggest you start making a list of your one Governing Principles that consists of your values, beliefs, and philosophy. For starters, I'll introduce you to three principles that I live by.

Governing Principle #1: Immunity To Criticism

If you were to summarise all the "Big Evil" reasons for why people fail, it would all come down to this single greatest human fear: **The Fear Of Being Judged.**

Most people fear the criticism of others. To be fair, being criticised is not a great feeling. Nobody wants to be told what they're doing is wrong or bad or stupid.

We want to feel accepted. Years of evolution have conditioned us to have an emotional need and want for acceptance.

Nobody initially wants to be an outcast. Nobody really sets out to be an outcast. Back in the day, if you were to deviate from the norms, or do "out of the ordinary things", or break the rules set by your village, you'd either be executed or exiled.

Left to fend for yourself. Looked down on, shunned upon, spat at, disrespected, humiliated. You were taught to stay in your lane or else.

Now this was back in those caveman and medieval years. It may have been true back then, but this way of living certainly isn't true for most of the world today—especially if you're living in a first-world capitalist country.

Today, if you study most successful people over the last 100 years, you'll notice that they've pretty much made up their own rules and have strayed from the norms set by others.

They've defied all the industry "norms" and followed what they believed was the best way forward. Elon Musk, Steve Jobs, all the mentors I gave credit to in an earlier chapter of this book.

Now this doesn't just apply to really big and wealthy entrepreneurs. This also applies for many of the "smaller" names—

mostly first generation "from-scratch" millionaires.

They do what makes them happy, hang out with people they like, say "yes" to the things they like, say "no" to things they don't like, and they laugh at and ignore everyone else who badmouths them.

If you've had some form of accomplishment in business, you know that it's a common experience to get criticism from others in your industry, typically competitors. They'll badmouth you in industry forums and complain about you on social media.

It's also common for some friends, relatives or family members to secretly be envious and try to diminish your success.

Realise that these things always happen to anyone who sets out to achieve anything significant in life and in business. When you get "big enough", there will come a point where people will inevitably judge you, criticise you, talk bad about you, tear you down—even if they don't know you.

That's simply the price you pay for success. **People who aren't successful (or at least making progress) WILL talk bad.** It's their way to feel better about their own failures, insecurities, and self-limiting beliefs.

Understand that those who tear others down and complain and gossip in industry forums and social media groups—they're technically losers. And you should feel sorry for them.

I mean, seriously? Name me one successful and influential person you know that has enough time to go on forums and social media groups to tear down other successful people in the industry?

NONE. Successful people don't have the time and energy to badmouth other successful people (at least not publicly). They're all too busy doing their own thing, finding ways to make more money, finding ways to enjoy their lives, finding ways to help more people, finding ways to become more successful.

On the other hand, if you choose to stay "small enough" by following the crowd and sticking to the rules like a good boy/girl, then you'd be more accepted by the village. Why? Because you aren't a threat.

The very thought of aspiring for more and greater achievement in life makes you a threat to the conformers. Being unsuccessful and somewhat of a failure makes you "just like them." You must always remember, people like people who are "just like them."

Losers hang out with losers. Winners hang out with winners. **Association matters**. A LOT.

So if you're striving for anything significant in life, you must learn to realise and accept that you WILL be criticised. You WILL be judged… but only by the people who aren't making any real progress in their lives; those who are stuck and miserable with their own reality. **It's the Price You Pay For Success.**

It doesn't mean you have to accept it. You can CHOOSE not to accept it. You can choose to design and create your life in any way you want. You're not bound by other people's opinion of you.

The only real opinion you should learn to accept is the opinion you have of yourself.

How do you see yourself? Do you accept yourself for who you are? Are you being your best authentic self?

My advice to anyone is to **always be your best self.** This is what will attract your people to you. Give yourself permission to let the real you out into the world and in business.

Personally, **I used to walk into a room and wonder if they liked me. Now I walk in and wonder if I like them.** If I don't, I'll see myself out of there. Life is too short to be associating yourself with people you don't like, and don't like you.

I'll end this lesson on *Immunity to Criticism* with a favourite story of mine from Lee Milteer.

Lee Milteer Story: You Are Not Everyone's Cup of Tea

As a very shy rancher's daughter growing up in the middle of nowhere, I came home from high school one day to find a mean-spirited letter in the mailbox from some female classmates. Their cruel words crushed me.

After moping around depressed for a couple of days, my dad took me horseback riding for a serious, grown-up conversation. He told me that I was different from the girls in high school, and I was never going to be everyone's cup of tea.

He did his best to explain that the world is filled with people who will simply not like me and will try to tear me down, no matter what I do, what I wear, or what I say.

But dad also told me, "The world is filled with people who will love you for being authentic. Those are your people.

"The best father's advice I could ever give you is to never be average and follow the crowds—they are weak-minded and easily manipulated. It takes nothing to join the crowd; it takes everything to stand your ground. You were born an original; don't change yourself so others will like you. You just be you and you will find your path in life just fine."

His advice has guided me for many years, particularly now during these unparalleled, polarised times. People have become sincerely afraid of just being their real selves, thanks to the daily media brainwashing that would have us all be politically correct, never saying or doing anything that might offend someone else. In business this is a death sentence.

How can you ever stand out in a crowd by being milk toast, blending in with everyone and everything around you?

So don't waste your time and emotional energy trying to convince people who are not aligned with you that you have value and worth. They will not buy what you are selling.

You are not their cup of tea, and they are not yours.

There is no need to pretend otherwise. Move away from them as fast as possible and don't look back.

Only share your path with those who clearly recognize and appreciate your gifts.

BE the original and authentic person you are.

There are plenty of people who will see your worth. Pay attention to your inner instincts and recognise those who are truly aligned with you and who are not, but often pretend to be if they can use you.

I am a very transparent kind of gal, so I'm finding these new, so-called rules very stifling to my own authentic, Red-Boots-wearing, tell-it-like-it-is personality. Of course, I have some sensitivity, but things have gone way too far.

I have decided not to play by others' rules (not that I did very much anyway). If you know me, this fact will not surprise you since I am known for truth-telling and having a Renegade personality.

So why is it that so many people are waiting to live their lives, go for their dreams, and express their true authentic selves in today's world?

The most exhausting thing in life is trying to please everyone. Life is too short to be living your life for the approval of others.

In one way or another, you're going to offend people. You're going to get judged and harshly criticised simply for existing.

It could be something about your hair, your nose, your accent, your skin colour, or because you look like the person their spouse cheated with. Whatever the reason, it doesn't matter and shouldn't matter to you. That's *their* problem. Not yours.

The thought that you're going to go through life without offending someone, never getting criticised—the only possible way to do that is to say nothing, do nothing, be nothing and die young— then MAYBE you won't be judged or criticised.

A wise man once told me…

"The world is full of people who wake up every day looking to get offended. I try my damndest not to disappoint them."

Governing Principle #2: The Majority Is ALWAYS Wrong

This idea originated with Earl Nightingale and later popularised by my mentor Dan Kennedy.

The premise is simple: **When it comes to making money and building wealth, the majority is always WRONG.**

A simple premise, yet very profound. It is vastly different from most people's thinking, attitudes and behaviour towards life.

Once you grasp this idea and start living it, it'll change your life forever—for the best. And I wholeheartedly mean that.

In his program, *Lead The Field*, Earl Nightingale said:

"If you had no successful example to follow in whatever endeavour you choose, you may simply look at what everyone else is doing and DON'T DO THAT. Do the opposite, because – THE MAJORITY IS ALWAYS WRONG."

This was one of the greatest discoveries I've ever come across when I first started out in business. It gave me the courage and permission to defy the "norms" I saw around me. It helped me realise that I didn't have to be just like everyone else.

From the very beginning, I've always had the feeling that the majority of people around me were completely and utterly clueless when it comes to living a meaningful life. They were all just pretending and winging everything as they went along.

Most people go through life going "whichever way the wind blows." They live their lives according to the thoughts, opinions, actions, desires or trends of other people—believing anything and everything the larger population and media tells them.

They don't take control of their lives. They're scared to think critically and responsibly. They fear standing out.

Maybe you've had that feeling too at some point in your life. Earl's teaching helped me validate this unspoken belief and gave me a much-needed boost of confidence and conviction. I hope my words here will do the same for you.

Let me give you an example to help illustrate this concept better.

In 1950s America, the Social Security Administration (who administers a social insurance program consisting of retirement, disability and survivor benefits) started tracking where people wound up from the beginning of their working lives (20 years old) up until the retirement age (which was 65 back then).

Here's what they found:

Introducing: THE MONEY PYRAMID

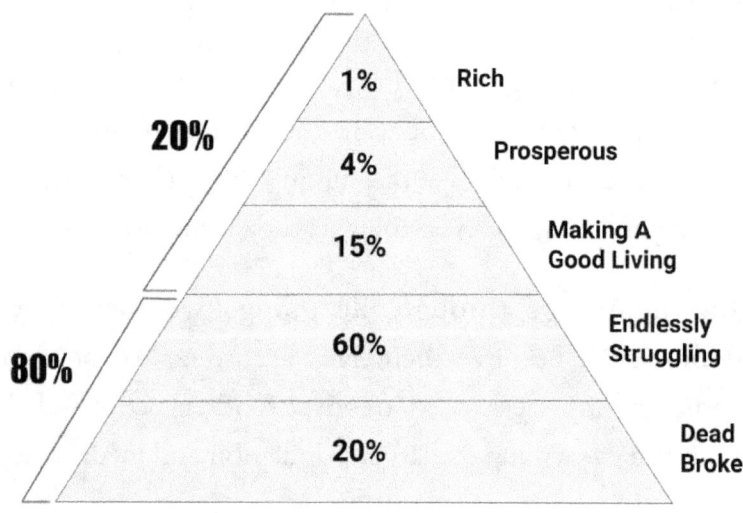

This applies to **ANY** group or population of individuals.

In our case, if we take any population of business owners or entrepreneurs, we'll find The Money Pyramid in effect regardless of the niche, industry or business we're in. 80% are either broke, endlessly struggling or "just getting by"... and 20% are living the good life, kicking butt and taking names.

Let's face it. It's hard to argue that you did much of anything right if you go through 45+ years of your working life and still wind up broke at age 65.

The Money Pyramid is true everywhere. It doesn't matter what type of group or population you gather. Take all the dentists or chiropractors or personal injury solicitors/lawyers in London and you'll see the same statistic… 80% are broke or struggling, 20% are succeeding.

It's even TRUER TODAY than it was back then. Think about it. **The access to information and advancement in technology has <u>not</u> changed this statistic** one bit.

Just think about the amount of information available today and the ease of access to them. If you don't know how to lift or do a squat safely, you can pull out your phone and simply Google or YouTube the answer.

If you don't know how to run a Facebook Ad, you can pull out your phone and search how to do it. You can even quickly find someone who can do it for you. If you don't know how to write a Sales Letter, you can pretty much do the same thing.

You don't have to get off your sofa, drive to the library and read a book anymore. It's all on your phone or laptop. All excuses for being broke are gone—especially if you live in a "first world" country. Information, ease of access, technology and opportunity are in abundance.

Yet the stats have not changed at all… and they NEVER

will! In fact, there's even MORE financial distress, overwhelm and confusion today.

How can this be? What makes the difference?

The reason why regardless of the external changes and advancement in information, technology, and ease of access don't work very well is because **The Money Pyramid is a reflection of people's <u>BEHAVIOUR</u>.**

People's quality of thinking, their attitudes and behaviour towards everything that has to do with living a meaningful and happy life is failing them. Whatever thinking or behaviour you see being "sold" to you by the majority must be approached with extreme caution.

In fact, when presented with a majority idea or opinion—particularly about money—you must laugh at that idea, reject it and avoid it like the plague. DO THE OPPOSITE.

If you want to be in the Top 5 Percent, the very first thing you must do is to NOT behave like the 95 Percenters.

<u>Here's a practical "To Do" exercise for you:</u>

1. Lock yourself in a quiet room, sit down and make a master list of all the "norms" and "how things are done around here" in your business, industry, profession.

2. Go through each item on your list and try to figure how to defy and violate each and every single one of them.

3. If you can't think of a legal way to violate an item, then at least make a commitment to yourself that you'll stop doing it. Do something else the majority aren't doing.

Once you start doing this, you'll immediately notice that you've pretty much aggravated a lot of people in your industry. You have a decision to make here. **Do you want your emotional need to be "accepted" met?**

Or do you want more money and time to provide for yourself and your family for generations to come? Which is more important to you?

The lead character in Arthur Miller's famous play *The Death of a Salesman*, Willy Loman, said these unfortunate words: "The most important thing is to be liked." Willy Loman never grew up.

His story is that of a modern tragedy. And it reflects most people's attitudes towards business. Hence why most people aren't successful. Most people get into business for all the wrong reasons—and one of those reasons is the need to be liked.

I advise you to get that idea out of your system. Business is about many things, but it is certainly NOT about being liked. Avoid disappointment and get that idea out of your head immediately.

Now, I understand that the challenge of being different and standing out from the crowd is quite immense. It's not actually a "real" challenge—more of an *emotional* obstacle you must overcome and embrace as the price you pay for wealth, success and autonomy.

Humans are inherently social creatures. For thousands of years, we learned that in order to survive, we must belong to a group and rely on other members.

Anyone who chooses to rebel and go against the "norms" is exiled and left to hunt, kill and provide for themselves.

Over time we developed a deep, emotional craving for being liked, recognised, and accepted by others. The desire to belong and be accepted in a group is a survival instinct ingrained into our very being.

This isn't to say that successful people don't belong in groups. They do. They join and contribute generously to a lot of smaller groups of like-minded individuals. However, they don't necessarily need to join any type of group in order to be a top performer.

They're very aware of who they are, what they want, and how they're going to do it. They never feel lost. If their organisations didn't exist, they would still thrive and be successful. It's who they are. It's their identity.

The point is this: Successful people don't need to rely on the majority opinions of "how things should be done around here." They have a mind of their own and they're not afraid to use it.

Remember:

If you want to succeed in any endeavour—and you don't know what to do, or don't have a model you can emulate— simply look at what everyone else is doing and DON'T DO

THAT. Do the Opposite. Because the majority is *always* WRONG, particularly about money and success.

If you want to be at the top of the Pyramid, you can't afford to behave like the 95 percenters.

Governing Principle #3: PRESS ON – "Nothing In The World Can take The Place Of Persistence"

How does a 52-year-old, constantly struggling milkshake machine salesman build a fast-food empire with 1,600 restaurants in 50 states, 5 foreign countries, with an annual revenue of in the neighbourhood of $700 million?

One word: Persistence.

Ray Kroc, the person responsible for what McDonald's is today, shared his philosophy on life and success back in the '60s or '70s, and in the 2016 movie *The Founder*.

Having faced countless rejections, risks and disappointments, he attributes his success to having the willingness and courage to *Press On* regardless of your current circumstance.

"Nothing in this world can take the place of good old Persistence.

Talent won't; nothing is more common than unsuccessful men with talent. Genius won't; unrewarded genius is practically a cliche. Education won't; why the world is full of educated fools.

Persistence and Determination alone are all powerful."

The problem with most business owners and entrepreneurs today is they are prone to **DABBLING.** They dabble and try a bunch of seemingly random ideas that aren't really grounded to a solid plan or strategy.

Most people who dabble often quit at the first sign of struggle; at the very first hurdle they encounter. **They don't commit to *mastering* any skill or craft.**

They lack discipline, determination and persistence. They don't have enough good reasons to "Press On."

Business owners are therefore often prime victims of charlatans who disguise themselves as "experts" selling and packaging their wares as the "new" bright shiny object.

This type of thing happens a lot on the internet. Lots of business owners, both new and established, are falling for the same old "newest 7-figure strategy that requires no skill, no money, no work, and no brains." Disgusting.

Let me tell you something. **There is <u>NOTHING</u> new under the sun.** Everything that works today has either been borrowed, stolen, re-purposed or re-packaged from what has been proven to work many, many years ago. DO NOT BE FOOLED.

The ideas and strategies in this very book are not new. I've borrowed many ideas from the names I've acknowledged at the very beginning of this book.

Today I continue to implement, help and teach other small business owners on what works today. My painful past experience diving into this whole "marketing thing" can be your shortcut to business success.

I've studied all the best and most powerful small business growth strategies—hundreds of books, courses, programs, articles, reports and newsletters—*so you don't have to.*

All I've done is I organised, repurposed and re-packaged it to fit the current market conditions in the small business arena today.

There is no need to be a pioneer and reinvent the wheel. Someone out there has already figured out what you want to achieve. All you have to do is study them, model them, try to emulate what they did to fit the current problems and challenges you're facing today.

Yes, it does take a bit of "thinking"—a foreign concept to most people, but that's life. You either deal with it or go get a job and let someone else decide how you live your life for you. That's reality.

Find someone (or better, find multiple people in different industries) that has already achieved what you want to achieve—or AT LEAST a few steps ahead of you—and emulate/model them.

Most importantly, when times get tough, PRESS ON and stick

with it. You will have to tweak your plan and strategies as you progress and gain more insights… but do not be deterred by bright shiny objects, designed to distract you from your long-term goals.

Another big reason why businesspeople lack the persistence and determination to see things through is because they have magically concocted more <u>EXCUSES</u> than reasons for doing well.

Most people tend to talk themselves out of things. They don't believe in themselves. They don't believe in what they are doing. They believe that everything is against them and they're hopelessly struggling to succeed.

Here's the truth about excuses: very few of us ever have it REALLY bad. This is a matter of _Perception VS. Perspective._

A lot of what you hear about people's reasons for not doing well aren't legitimate reasons at all; they are simply excuses to justify their lack of progress or success.

I remember an old story about a guy named Roger who was in the Amway business. (selling health, beauty and home care products). Roger had been paralysed and confined to a wheelchair due to a trampoline accident.

His two greatest (remaining) tools: a good speaking voice and an unwavering determination to not let his permanent physical condition define the rest of his life.

50

He had no connections and was too poor to hire someone to assist him with what most people would define as "simple" tasks. He started each day cold calling. "Dialing for dollars", pushing phone buttons with a pencil clutched to his teeth.

He eventually built up a customer base generating over $10,000 a month. He hired a delivery guy and a personal assistant to help improve operations and productivity. He climbed up the "ladder of levels", went on award cruises and made enough money to pay off his mortgage and even have his house remodelled.

I find a lot of people have an almost never-ending list of "reasons" for why they can't or won't succeed.

None of those items on their list includes having to accept being permanently put in a wheelchair for the rest of their lives, starting each day cold calling, pushing buttons using the pencil clutched to their teeth.

Most people's perception of a bad day is waking up to the sound of their alarm. Think about that. Most business owners' perception of a bad day is when I hear things like "Yeah but… my employees won't do that"... or "too bad this won't work for me, I live in a really small town"... or "Big major corporation XYZ has come to my area and I simply can't compete."

A bunch of excuses for not doing well. So what's the solution here? Should we all just quit then? Should we curl up into a foetal position and cry?

Understand that many of the millionaires, multi-millionaires, even billionaires you see today (and throughout history) started with nothing, from nothing. They had their own set of struggles and obstacles they had to overcome in order to raise themselves up from nothing to something.

If you study any "from-scratch" millionaire—inside or outside your field, doesn't matter—what you'll find is they've all set aside their "Book of Excuses." They got rid of their list of reasons for not doing well and replaced that list with reasons <u>for</u> doing well.

Few people are attracted to whiners, complainers, excuse-makers and wimps. Hanging out with a victim is not appealing. Nobody wants to be involved with an emotional cripple.

Money is attracted by taking responsibility and is repelled by making excuses. The habit of excuse making is the worst of all habits.

How to Reinforce the Attitude of Persistence

1. Set aside your "Book of Excuses" once and for all

2. Replace that list with "All The Good Reasons To Succeed."

3. Avoid distractions. Avoid dabbling. Beware of shiny objects. Beware of peddlers of shiny objects.

4. Make the deliberate Decision to Succeed and ***stick with it.***

Don't be like that miner who was "3 Feet From Gold." A story during the Gold Rush of a young man who spent months mining for gold, only to quit just before he struck gold. He sold all his equipment and machinery to a junkman.

The junkman wasn't convinced that the mine had no gold, so he sought expert advice from a mining engineer. After careful inspection, the engineer found that the vein of gold ore was just 3 feet away from where the miner had stopped drilling.

If you want to succeed, you must develop the stamina and the remarkable determination to see things through and *"Press On."*

SECTION TWO

How To Solve ALL Your Marketing & Advertising Problems Once and For All!

Chapter 3: Why Everything You've Been Told To Believe About Marketing & Advertising Your Small Business Is WRONG

Before we get into the nuts and bolts of how to create an effective marketing strategy and system for your business, there is one thing you have to do.

You must **UNLEARN** just about everything you've been taught and conditioned to believe about growing your business. Remember, the majority is ALWAYS wrong—particularly about things that have to do with money and success.

So whatever the majority are doing whenever they attempt to grow their businesses, attract more customers, make more sales, get more and better leads, schedule more appointments etc., the first thing that has to come to your mind is "I better not do that."

It doesn't really matter yet if you don't know what to do. What matters more in the beginning is to accept the fact that whatever the majority in your field are doing is ineffective. The evergreen statistics (Money Pyramid) tell us that they are screwed up, ineffective and wildly unprofitable.

You see, you have been <u>lied to</u>... for a very long time!

If you are a small business owner today, you are extremely confused and overwhelmed. That's by design. You have not been "misinformed" or "told inaccurate information." No. LIED TO.

If you weren't confused, overwhelmed and feeling inadequate, you wouldn't be a prime target for business-building vultures and marketing agency salespeople to prey on. It's important to your success to understand this truth and be aware of it.

Because what I'm about to share with you in this section of the book will open your eyes to a radically different and counterintuitive way of acquiring customers, clients, patients, and boosting sales and profits.

The fact of the matter is, you are sick and tired of so-called experts and their conflicting opinions about how you should grow your business.

You're getting hammered on all sides with "gurus" telling you to do one thing or another; doing a bunch of random and erratic marketing activities that hardly moves the needle.

Like a hamster on a wheel, you feel like you have to do more; to run faster and faster—only to get the same little results. Or less.

And like many other serious business owners, entrepreneurs, and sales professionals, you've probably tried marketing.

Spent serious money on advertising that didn't sell anything, SEO that takes decades to see profitable results, "funnels" that under delivered or drained your bank account dry—and probably tried a host of other approaches, none of which delivered the results promised or expected.

I am here to help you—to mute all the noise and guide you to clarity on a relatively short list of principles and strategies (not short-term fads).

When you "get it", you'll have a system that feeds you new customers, clients or patients on a predictable basis. You will never feel the anxiety of wondering when or where your next customer is coming from. In fact, you'll finally be able to take a break or go on holiday without checking your phone every hour.

But as I said at the beginning of this chapter, before you can begin to do anything with marketing, you must first UNLEARN everything you've been told to believe about how to market and grow your business.

I have identified **SIX major "big picture" reasons why most small business marketing and advertising fails.** All have to do with myths and false beliefs. Let's go through each one.

Mistake #1: "Build It And They Will Come"

This relates to the idea that if you build the best product, deliver the best service, have the best location, be the most skilled person in your craft, "they" (your customers, clients or patients) will somehow notice and therefore beat a path to your door.

If you study the history of the business you're in, you'll discover that this was certainly true back in the day. If you opened up a restaurant in your community back in the 1950's, you'd certainly get all or at least the majority of the customers in your area. Why? Because **you're the <u>ONLY ONE.</u>**

Back then, there was only one restaurant in town, one dental clinic, one chiropractic clinic, one financial planning firm, one law firm, one car dealership, one estate agency... you get the idea. One of everything within a small geographic or local area.

Back then, you could wake up one day, decide to start a small business, rent a physical space, put a sign out saying, "We're Open", and customers would flock to your door. **<u>Fact:</u> You had either very little or zero competition because you were the only one.**

Today, this concept of "build it and they will come" is far from the truth. It is, in fact, a big and costly mistake. You can find a restaurant almost anywhere and everywhere. There are even small, local burger and pizza shops right next to each other.

There are three estate agencies right across the street from each other. There are numerous car dealerships, dental clinics, chiropractic clinics and law firms in your town or city right now.

And we're only talking local here. If you do business on a regional or national scale, the Internet has made it even tougher for you to cut through the noise and clutter.

Consider the battle for people's attention today. If you're not doing everything you can possibly do to stay in front of your ideal customers, clients or patients, then you are simply "out of sight, out of mind."

If you're not constantly promoting your business; if you do not have a reliable, dependable marketing system in place to predictably generate a steady stream of high-quality leads, appointments and buyers, then you'll be forced to rely on hope.

Hoping, waiting, wishing, praying and worrying where your next customer will come from. A wise elder once told me that **there is nothing gained by being the best-kept secret in town.**

Build it and they will come? I think not. Today the formula is more like:

1. Identify a nagging **PROBLEM** in the marketplace

2. Find or create the **SOLUTION** (doesn't have to be perfect from the start—test a "prototype" or a "minimum viable"

product, service or solution)

3. Build a **SYSTEM** to advertise and promote the solution

4. And only then, **"they" will they come**

Most skip #3. Mistake. This brings me to another major business error, which somewhat links to this one...

Mistake #2: Marketing Viewed as a "Necessary Evil"

Willie Sutton was an infamous bank robber who had an affinity for expensive clothes. He was added to the FBI's Ten Most Wanted list in 1950. He was also arrested a number of times throughout his career as a bank robber, and even managed to escape from prison six times.

When asked by a reporter why he chooses to rob banks, Sutton replied, *"Because that's where the money is."*

Regardless of his chosen career, Sutton was a shrewd businessman. **In business, the smart and profitable companies are the ones that focus heavily on the** marketing **of the business—because** *that's where the money is.*

If you think of Apple, who's the first person that comes to mind? Steve Jobs. If you study Apple and how they came to dominate their space, you'll find that not only did they have a great product, Jobs was also a brilliant and relentless marketer.

You can find many Steve Jobs presentations and Apple advertising campaigns on YouTube. It'll be instructive for your own education and entertainment to watch them.

Jobs understood that having a great product was simply not enough. It must be combined with the smart planning and execution of marketing and advertising campaigns in order to separate themselves from the crowd of tech geeks and position themselves as the one and only solution their target audience needs.

Unfortunately, most small business owners don't know where the money is. They still think it's in the DO-ing of their "thing."

They are still stuck in the outdated 1900's belief that if you simply get better at the DO-ing of whatever it is you sell, you're bound to get rich, be successful and live a great lifestyle others would envy.

That may be true back in the old days. Today however, nothing could be further from the truth.

You see, most businesspeople are stuck. They go into business for all the **wrong reasons.** When a person starts a business, they often do it because they simply want to be a DO-er of their "thing" without having an "idiot boss" to bow down to.

Most business owners often get their start by serving only the small number of customers referred to them by friends, family, or just so happens to stumble upon them by chance.

They view marketing, advertising, and promoting their business as a necessary evil. They don't want to sell. They don't want to promote.

They feel some sort of entitlement. They mistakenly believe that because they've worked so hard to start their own business, and they're somewhat "good" at what they do, customers should notice them, do business with them and give them money.

Well guess what? There's A LOT of people who are "good" at their craft out there.

Most of them don't get noticed or simply ignored by the marketplace. There's more to business than just being good at what you do. Being "good" is just the ante to playing the game.

Let's face it. *If your business, product or service was so damn good, why shouldn't you market it?*

If you are better than the rest of your competition, then why hold back? It's your moral and professional obligation to let the people you can help know about you.

It's the fastest way to stand out from the crowd and leave your competition in the dust. Your aim should be to become the one true King (or Queen) in your category.

So if your product or service is so good and you want to accelerate your success, don't stay quiet. Promote.

Please be very smart about this. Decide today that you'll eliminate any queasiness and false beliefs you feel about anything that has to do with marketing, advertising and sales. These are the most important functions in business today.

Nothing happens until somebody <u>buys</u>.

Marketing, especially the style of marketing I'm going to teach you, helps facilitate sales and eliminates the majority of sales and price resistance in the actual "selling" event.

Mistake #3: Confusing MEDIA With MARKETING

The biggest mistake business owners make when investing in marketing is **jumping straight to media decisions rather than marketing <u>strategy</u> decisions.**

When business owners think about marketing, they only think about which media channel to use and invest time and money in. They ask themselves questions like "Should I be on Facebook, Instagram, Google, TikTok?" and "Should I do direct mail—leaflets, flyers, postcards?"

They don't think about the actual plan and strategy that will govern every marketing decision and investment they'll make now and into the future.

They're asking the wrong questions. **They confuse Media with Marketing.** They've been led to believe that the media channel itself (Facebook, Instagram, Google, SEO, YouTube, TikTok,

Email, Postcard etc.) is what marketing is.

And pretty much everyone in their industry, including competitors, think this way.

Wrong, wrong, wrong.

Media is NOT Marketing. It is only <u>ONE out of the THREE</u> building blocks for effective marketing. This distinction is extremely important.

It is where most people wind up spending tens of thousands on marketing only to later find out they're not getting any real results—even after throwing money at some online media channel they've been sold as the "magic bullet."

We'll talk more about how to choose the right Media for you to invest in a later chapter. For now, you must be very wary about so-called experts and marketing agencies trying to sell you on throwing money at any media channel.

Think about it. **The only reason they're trying to convince you to invest in a certain type of media channel is because they're SELLING it.**

Media decisions must be governed by a **carefully planned strategy.** You must never invest any amount of time, money or resources on a media channel just because someone (media salesperson, competitor, staff or peer) said you should.

Mistake #4: No Marketing SYSTEM

Keyword: **System.** A big reason why most small business marketing "doesn't work" is **because there is no systemised process for attracting ideal leads and buyers—consistently, predictably, and profitably.**

As I said above, most business owners often jump to media choices and call it marketing.

They build a website, set up their social media pages, post randomly online, set up their Google stuff, maybe pay a small sum to boost a post on Facebook, maybe send out a few leaflets or flyers within a small radius around their location.

That's it. That's what most small business owners do and that's the idea they've been sold to believe by certain fake gurus, marketing agencies and media salespeople.

In other words, they do **random and erratic acts of *attempted* marketing. There's no SYSTEM in place that focuses on a clear process for:**

1. **Getting a lead**

2. **Turning that lead into a call, enquiry or appointment**

3. **Converting that appointment into a customer**

At a minimum, you want a **Lead-Generation and Customer-Acquisition Marketing System** that focuses on the three key areas above.

You want to **<u>OWN</u>** and **<u>CONTROL</u>** a system that consistently and predictably feeds new leads and buyers to you whenever you want. Think of it as like a faucet you can turn on or off, up or down, depending on the needs of your business.

The danger of not having the right Marketing System is the fact you'll one day be forced to rely on hope. When times are tough (which is certainly true at the time of this writing) and customers are scarce, **you are forced to do marketing out of fear and sheer desperation to survive.**

And because your marketing efforts reek of neediness and desperation, you repel customers instead of attracting them.

You'll tend to talk more about yourself and how great you are rather than talking about how you can help your customers and be of value to them. You're more prone to falling victim to the sweet overpromises of fake gurus and marketing agency salespeople.

You're forced to throw everything into your marketing efforts, hoping and praying for a "one-hit wonder"—something that worked once or twice or for a short period of time, but you don't know why, and you have no idea how to do it again. Once it's gone, it's gone.

On the flipside, **once you have a Marketing System set up, you can simply turn it on or off as you please. You can set it in motion and it'll work for you 24/7, 365.**

It is an **<u>ASSET</u>**. Think of it as a cash-generating machine you invest in once and can have it running for years and years—consistently generating new leads and buyers on a predictable basis.

Remember: Random acts of marketing lead to RANDOM cash flow, RANDOM income, RANDOM success. You don't want to stumble upon random and fragile success that you won't be able to replicate. You want *consistent* and *predictable* success.

Having a real marketing SYSTEM in place frees you up from doing one random thing you do at random times... to having 20 profit-generating things you do consistently that gets predictable results, and barely having to lift a finger.

Mistake #5: Blindly Delegating and Abdicating Control Of Your Marketing Over To "Experts" (Coaches, Consultants, Marketing & Ad Agencies)

The typical businessperson today receives a never-ending amount of unsolicited advice from "experts" eager to offer their opinions and services—for a price. These include coaches, consultants, marketing and ad agencies.

Renowned speaker Bill Brooks once said that the definition of a "consultant" is someone who knows 357 sexual positions but can't get a date.

He may have said it jokingly, but there's some truth to it, and a very accurate description of most experts and consultants today.

The truth about these "experts" is the fact there are barely any that actually does for themself what they claim to be able to help you with.

In other words, **most people who claim to be experts at marketing your business simply don't and don't know how to market and advertise their OWN services.** A very obvious fact, yet most people don't see it.

Look, I get it. It's a natural thing to look for a wizard. For someone to hand the whole thing off to and say, "Just deliver me leads, appointments and sales, I'll stand back and wait."

Realise that when you give that responsibility and control away, you have very few options of who to give it to.

Frankly, **most of the agencies and so-called gurus who will take your money for it are really not qualified to make marketing decisions about your business.** Not nearly as qualified as you are to make those choices.

Let me tell you a dirty little secret about most marketing and ad agencies: they hire outside sales consultants to help them craft presentations to pitch to new potential clients. Why? Because **without outside help, they can't sell their own services!**

Other than that, the other big marketing "strategy" most marketing/ad agencies use to get clients is they build a huge list of business emails using tools that scrape email addresses from the deep, dark web.

They then send cold email blasts to these "leads" (not really leads, as they didn't consent to receiving any marketing communication) hoping and praying someone would be desperate enough to have a conversation with them.

Ironically, this is how most "lead generation companies" would try to generate your own "leads" for you.

Absolute fools. I already feel dirty just writing the above paragraph. I don't care what anybody says, that is NOT marketing.

That is spam and being a little annoying pest. Most of these people lack integrity, lack real business knowledge, and certainly lack real expertise.

The only person who is a 100% true expert about marketing your business is you. YOU are your own best guru.

Think about it. You already know more about your business than anybody else. If you know or even have an idea about WHO your best customers are and WHAT results they want from you, then you already have two out of the three sides of the "Marketing Results Triangle" right.

You don't need to waste outrageous sums of money on the newest shiny objects and media platforms that the gurus are throwing at you. Those things come and go, fast.

As said earlier, what you really need is to equip yourself with a customised SYSTEM to get more and better customers, clients or patients at a predictable rate.

This way, **you can <u>OWN</u> your marketing.** Once you have a system in place, you can hire others to do all the technical stuff and all you have to do is manage and maintain the system.

At the very least, you can create a marketing system for yourself and then hand it off to a marketing agency to implement for you.

But you should NEVER blindly abdicate the responsibility and control of the vital process of getting qualified leads and buyers to some wizard. Especially some greasy internet wizard.

The big mistake made with blindly offloading your marketing & advertising to some wizard is the fact that most businesspeople tend to jump from one (hopefully) quick-fix solution, one magic answer, one so-called expert… to another.

All while paying extortionately high fees along the way, but never getting the results they were promised.

Blind reliance on wizards, slick-talking online gurus, and marketing agencies is the fastest way to stay stuck, confused, overwhelmed and struggling in this new economy.

They will drag you down endless rabbit holes and shove the next new nonsensical fad strategy down your throat.

Their true goal is to keep you feeling <u>inadequate</u> and therefore <u>dependent</u> on them.

If you're looking for marketing firms to hand over your marketing to, be very careful, because:

THEIR agenda is <u>not</u> YOUR agenda.

<u>Here's what THEIR agenda looks like</u> (I encourage you to do some research and prove to yourself if this list is accurate):

1. How to get clients and outsource it to someone from India or the Philippines for the minimum amount possible (£2.50 or $3.20 an hour). OR hire somebody fresh out of university to handle client accounts. Yikes!

2. Winning awards (Just look at their websites)

3. Creative Concerns

4. Peer approval

5. Building their portfolio

6. Media commission

7. Mark ups

8. Satisfy the biases of their superiors

9. Satisfy the client's preconceived ideas

10. Going on marketing-related Facebook groups and asking, "How do I get more clients?"

11. Client results

<u>Now, here's what YOUR agenda looks like:</u>

1. Results

2. Results

3. Results

Specifically, **<u>measurable</u> results:** in leads, calls, appointments, sales, buyers, money. NOT likes, comments, shares, views, impressions, "engagement."

As you can see, regardless of what they tell you, your results aren't even in their top ten list of priorities. Don't believe me? Look at their websites and see how they love to brag about their awards for "most creative agency" and a ton of other fluffy, nonsense, egotistical awards that no client ever cares about.

Notice how there's no award for "The agency that made their client the MOST MONEY from their campaign." They value stroking their egos more than getting their clients real results.

They care about their egos more than freeing you up from your business worries, so you can actually spend more time with your kids or grandchildren—and actually *be there* mentally, without having to worry about your business, wondering when and where your next customer will come from.

The number one thing you can do right now to set you apart from all the rest of the "me too" competitors out there is to **STOP abdicating your marketing to wizards and so-called experts. You must take back control and OWN your marketing.**

Yes, you can do it. It's easier than you think. You don't have to actually do the technical stuff of marketing. Quite frankly, I hate doing the technical stuff myself. I get lost easily in technology and it just isn't for me.

What I mean by "Owning Your Marketing" is you must take back control and responsibility of the part of your business that gets leads, customers, clients or patients IN the door.

That means you should take the time to educate yourself and your team on the best way to market and promote your business to your ideal prospects.

And ultimately, invest in creating a dependable marketing SYSTEM which you can then delegate to marketing agencies, outside consultants, or hire an in-house marketing person/team to implement and manage for you.

But you must **never become dependent on the cookie-cutter solutions devised by marketing/ad agencies themselves.**

Otherwise you'll be forced to rely on someone else's system and be pigeon-holed into the "same old, same old" methods that most of your copycat competitors are using—which is a surefire way to NOT stand out from the crowd.

You'd just be another **optional and fragile** business competing on lowest price to attract the lowest quality, price-driven, difficult and high maintenance customers.

Mistake #6: "Monkey See, Monkey Do" Marketing

What do most people do when they first get into business? **They look around at what everybody else is doing and try to blindly copy it—but only to try to do it better. Not radically different, just a little bit better.**

What happens in any field or industry is this: Everybody stands in a circle looking at each other, copying each other, and ignoring everyone and everything outside that circle. This is particularly true for just about any business category you can think of.

If you're in, say, the restaurant business, chances are you go to restaurant owner association meetings and conventions, you read restaurant industry magazines, you pay close attention to other restaurants' advertising, and so on.

You copy other restaurant owners. Other restaurant owners copy you. And before you know it, you (and everyone else in your industry) are guilty of committing MARKETING INCEST. Pretty soon, everyone around you is as dumb as a rock.

Don't miss it. I'm only using the restaurant industry to illustrate this reality. Look at your own industry. You'll notice this also applies to you. It's part of human nature.

Problem is, the only kind of improvement you can make in this scenario are all minor and incremental gains—at best.

At worst, you could easily throw away large sums of money,

energy and resources trying to copy people in your industry without fully understanding why they're doing what they're doing.

So everybody's just trying to do what everyone else is doing, simply trying to do a little bit better. That's why nobody stands out.

In your ideal prospect's mind, you're all the same and there's nothing truly unique or significant that distinguishes one from the other.

Here's the Big Secret about this:

Breakthroughs Come From <u>Outside</u> The Business, Not Inside.

Major breakthroughs come from taking what's already working outside of your industry, taking it back to yours and applying it for yourself. Read that again.

Here are a couple of examples that might be familiar to you.

Federal Express adapted what's called a hub-and-spoke distribution system which enabled them to deliver packages overnight. This concept was originally taken from the banking industry—where they sent all checks to a central processing point, then out to the appropriate branch.

George Thomas, the inventor of the roll-on deodorant, was trying to find a more convenient and effective way for people to apply deodorant.

Little did he know that he was already holding the answer right in his hand. He got the idea for roll-on technology by examining how ink flowed from a ballpoint pen onto the paper.

Similarly, marketing and financial breakthroughs occur when an entrepreneur stops what the majority in their industry is doing, goes outside and brings something back from a different industry.

In this book, I'll show you a completely different way of marketing your business, a contrarian approach to creating power for yourself in a cluttered marketplace.

I'm here to dare you to turn back on the incestuous "monkey see, money do" circle and have the courage to do the opposite of what everybody else is doing. Go in search of something different.

Not just "a little bit better," but different in ways of marketing your business to stand out from the crowd and cut through the overwhelming noise and clutter of me-too messages.

The Quantum Leap To Greater Income & Results: From Do-er Of The "Thing" To MARKETER Of The "Thing"

Back then, the only requirement you needed to achieve greater income and success was to become a better do-er of whatever thing you're selling.

Ralph Waldo Emerson once said, "If you build a better

mousetrap, the world will beat a path to your door." This no longer applies in the business world today.

In this day and age, anybody can find lots of good mouse traps. It's no longer about just building a "better" mousetrap.

It's now about being a better MARKETER of the mousetrap—even if it's not the best in the marketplace (though it's an advantage if you are the best, or at least very good).

The best marketers of the product, service or "thing" are often the most successful businesses.

Again, look at Apple. Steve Jobs wasn't just a great innovator, he was a brilliant marketer. Without his iconic presentations, his ability to persuade, his commitment to market and sell the iPhone and other Apple products, then Samsung would be the world's top smartphone seller today.

Everybody falsely believes that the thing they DO is the business. Not anymore. What's true today and what you've got to get in your head is the fact that:

Marketing IS The Business

If you ask most people what they do or what business they're in, they'll describe it in a way that a shopkeeper would describe it.

So if you walk into a printing shop and ask the owner "what do you do?", he'll probably give you a blank look and say, "Well, I provide printing services." If you ask a restaurant owner the same question, he'll say "I serve delicious food to people."

This is pretty much how most business owners think. If you ask them what they do at a cocktail party, they'll give you a shopkeeper type of answer focusing on the deliverable—the product or service.

This stems from the false belief that most business owners are mired in. The belief that being a DO-er of your thing and being a "better" DO-er will somehow bring you more customers, clients or patients. They view marketing as either a supplementary task or a necessary evil.

If you want to increase your earning potential and dominate your chosen market, you cannot afford to accept this attitude.

There are countless business owners who are great at what they do, but don't achieve the same level of success in the BUSINESS of what they do.

If you look at the most successful "from-scratch" high income entrepreneurs today, you'll see that they've flipped this false belief upside down. They took the quantum leap and went from being DO-er of their thing, to being a MARKETER of their thing.

They see marketing as the most important, exciting and enjoyable part of business. They love the feeling of acquiring leads and buyers on a consistent and predictable basis.

So they view marketing as their primary role—with the actual doing or fulfilment of the product/service as a secondary task or even a necessary evil.

The breakthrough shift that you must make today is to go from being just a "doer" of your product or service—to becoming a <u>marketer</u> of your product or service.

Understand that you are NOT in the business of DOING the "thing." You are in the business of MARKETING the "thing."

Why? **Because there is no business without qualified leads, prospects, customers, clients or patients to present your "thing" to.**

The ability to get something sold is the highest-value skill on earth. Once you can market one thing effectively, you can market anything effectively—even in a down economy.

And *that* is reassuring. You will never run out of opportunities to raise yourself up and earn a good living if you are willing and know how to market.

If you "get it" but you know you're not going to be engaging as much in marketing due to a very busy schedule, you must at least learn what good marketing looks like, so you can delegate the specific implementation of marketing tasks onto others.

But you should never just blindly offload and give up control and responsibility of your marketing so-called experts and wizards —especially the planning and strategy.

NEVER place your trust in the incompetence of most marketing/advertising agencies. They, too, don't know what they're doing. How can people who don't know how to market themselves ever have a chance of marketing yours?

You must <u>OWN</u> your marketing and devise a carefully engineered <u>SYSTEM</u> that gets you consistent and predictable new business while you sleep.

Once you have a system in place, you can easily hire others to do all the technical stuff and all you have to do is manage and maintain the system.

Chapter 4: The Two Worlds Of Advertising

To quote the Father of Advertising, David Ogilvy, "There are two worlds in advertising..."

My world of **Direct Response Advertising:** advertising to elicit a measurable response...

And the world of **Traditional Advertising:** where most brand-focused and image-related advertising occur (like the Coca-Cola and McDonald's ads you see on bus stops and billboards).

The world of mainstream traditional "brand" and "image" advertising is where a lot of largely unaccountable advertising and marketing takes place. Most of the money invested in it is based on blind faith and hope.

As an aside, you should know that there's a distinct difference between an "image" ad and a "brand" ad. Image ads are the worst because they have no strategic purpose whatsoever apart from looking pretty.

Brand ads often use images but are geared more towards promoting the brand than anything else. For convenience, we'll refer to both as "Traditional Advertising."

Unfortunately, this is the type of advertising you see used by most small and local businesses. They blindly copy ads that focus more on the brand and image—bright lights, pretty pictures, big logos, clever slogans and taglines.

Think about the ads you see on billboards, TV and buses. These big corporations and their ad agencies are focused on and more worried about their "brand image."

They're running ads for totally different reasons, such as pleasing their investors and board of directors (most of whom know zip about how to get customers in the door but have lots of opinions) than actually getting a return on investment on their ad spend.

It is my firm belief that advertising is an expense unless and until it's able to prove a return on investment (ROI).

Real results that can be measured in the form of: number of leads, quality of leads, number of calls, appointments, new customers, gross sales or net profit.

For this reason, I made the conscious decision to master my craft in the world of ***Direct Response Marketing & Advertising***, where a smaller and smarter group of unapologetic rebels and nonconformists choose to live.

It's based on a simple premise: **for every pound or dollar invested, there is a direct, typically fast, and always measurable return on investment PLUS some profit (now or forecasted sometime in the future).**

You can boil it down to two very basic ideas:

1. **Invest £1 in marketing, get back £2 to £20 (or more)— FAST.** That may be within a few hours, the next day, a few days, in a week, or a month. Either way, you won't have to wait and hope for ten months or even years wondering whether your advertising is profitable or not.

2. **Do NOT spend £1 on any marketing or advertising that does not directly and quickly bring back £2 or more.**

The big difference between traditional advertising and direct response advertising is this: **deliberate enticement of <u>response</u>.**

To get a response, you need to **present your audience with an Irresistible Offer**, which we'll talk more about in a later chapter. Compare this to traditional advertising, which presents no offer or method of response. Just clever words and pretty pictures.

Small businesses blindly copy traditional advertising because it's what they see big, dumb companies do. It's a mistake because unlike big corporations, small businesses don't have an infinite supply of other people's money to play with.

Small business advertising cannot wait years and years for

"brand awareness" to kick in. What they need is some form of measurable return on investment NOW or very close to now, otherwise they won't be in business for long.

Many big corporations and their ad agencies who do traditional advertising for them worship at the altar of "creativity." They usually come up with a smart and clever slogan combined with a fancy-looking artwork, image, or video.

Then they throw a truckload of investors' money to place the ad on a billboard. This consequently puts their ad in front of thousands of unqualified, and mostly uninterested eyes.

How do they know if their advertising is working? They don't. They wait. Hoping and praying they'll get some piece of the market pie. They don't track or measure any meaningful number that might prove whether or not their advertising is working.

Traditional advertising is a form of advertising based on hope. It's all about hopefully getting an interested prospect to notice you.

Hopefully getting them to leave all their plans behind to call or book an appointment. Hopefully enticing them to stop whatever they're doing in their busy schedules and pull out their wallets and buy. A nice thought? Sure. Realistic? No.

The quickest way to waste money in advertising is to do it the way big, dumb companies do it: Name, logo, clever slogan, fancy image, maybe a phone number, maybe a website, throw other people's money at it, then HOPE.

They can afford to do this because they're not using their own hard-earned money. They have bottomless pockets filled with other people's money.

Traditional advertising works for them because of the power of Repetition.

After many years, they'll be able to somehow recoup some of their advertising investment due to people's increased awareness and familiarity with them. So they're not worried about making any sales or profits from their ads any time soon.

What they hope to accomplish with the repetition of their ads is that one day, when a prospect reaches the point of being ready to buy, they will hopefully remember that big, dumb company.

For a small business to try and copy this model is an incredibly futile and wasteful exercise. You must get a RETURN on investment as fast as possible. Otherwise you'll be in trouble.

As a small business owner, you cannot afford to wait years and years for advertising to yield a financial return; you cannot afford to waste even a single penny on unaccountable, hope-based marketing & advertising. You want and need results NOW.

This is what direct response is about. Direct Response Marketing & Advertising is:

The practice of communicating an OFFER...

directly to a pre-selected, pre-defined AUDIENCE...

and supplying the method for a RESPONSE.

This is very different from the brand and image advertising you see most people do, like the Pepsi TV commercial or the McDonald's banner ads on bus stops that don't include a specific request for a response or way to measure results.

The No B.S. Truth: The typical business owner is essentially clueless when it comes to advertising and marketing.

This makes them highly vulnerable to being preyed on by media salespeople, marketing agencies, social media wizards, slick-talkers, fake "gurus" and other industry vultures.

They are, therefore, often *Advertising Victims*—easy prey for charlatans and peddlers of shiny objects who don't know anything about how to market, advertise and promote a small business any more than they do.

If you think I'm wrong, try this: If you can corner one of your peers, try to get him to tell you with confidence where his customers are coming from, what it costs to get them, and what kind of results one ad gets versus another. Try. He'll look at you like a deer in headlights.

This confusion is what the marketing & advertising industry vultures rely on. They know that when their client can only GUESS how well their marketing and advertising works, they have a credit card they can ding regularly and without fail.

Industry vultures rely on two lethal weapons to keep you dependent on them:

1. **Convince you to pay big money to "get your brand out there" and do unmeasurable traditional, brand and image-based advertising.** This is what most marketing firms and agencies rely on... Or the more modern weapon, used by most so-called gurus online:

2. **Confuse and overwhelm you with shiny objects, quick fix solutions, and magic bullets**... one after the other... *so you feel inadequate* and choose to give up the responsibility of your marketing to them.

Either way, they get paid. You stay confused and out of pocket until you realise how little results they're getting for you and move on to the next marketing agency or bright new shiny object.

My goal and promise to you is that when you're done reading and studying this book, you will no longer feel inadequate. **Think of this book as your go-to marketing manual—your small business marketing BIBLE.**

You'll finally be able to build and own a marketing system that brings you new leads, appointments, and ready-to-buy prospects at a consistent and predictable rate.

A system you can rely on to get more high-quality, high value customers, clients or patients to your door. Customers who are more open and willing to accept your propositions because they see you as a trusted advisor instead of just another salesperson desperate to sell them stuff.

Here, I'll provide you with a list of "commandments" to follow for now, until you're ready to go out and experiment new ideas for yourself.

Any marketing and advertising you do from now on will revolve around these following **10 No B.S. Direct Response Marketing Commandments**, as taught by my mentor and marketing legend, Dan Kennedy:

The 10 No B.S. Rules of Successful Direct Response Marketing

1. **There shall always be an OFFER(S).** Make every communication ask your audience to do something. You accomplish this by presenting them with an Irresistible Offer they simply cannot refuse.

2. **There shall always be a REASON TO RESPOND NOW.** The biggest hidden cost and failure in all advertising and marketing is with the "almost persuaded" prospects— who noticed your message, wanted to respond, but then chose to set it aside to "do later." But "later" never comes.

3. **There shall always be CLEAR INSTRUCTIONS on HOW TO RESPOND.** Confused prospects do nothing. People rarely act on anything or buy anything of consequence without being asked. Most failures result from giving vague directions, confusing directions or no directions at all.

4. **There shall be TRACKING, MEASUREMENT, and ACCOUNTABILITY.** Never invest in any advertising or marketing that doesn't allow you to track and measure results that matter: leads, calls, appointments, customers, and money/return on investment.

5. **Brand-Building will be a HAPPY BY-PRODUCT of direct response marketing, NOT the other way round.** As you do direct response marketing, you'll simultaneously build the power of your brand because your audience will start to notice you and pay attention to you. Get response first, then gratefully accept brand-building as a bonus.

6. **NEVER do one-step marketing. There shall always be FOLLOW-UP.** When you invest in marketing and advertising, you don't just pay for the customers you get, you pay a price for every website visit, every phone call, every inquiry. Doing nothing with these "unconverted leads" is flushing money down the toilet.

7. **There shall always be strong SALES COPY (i.e. Copywriting).** There is enormous, ever-growing and overwhelming competition for the attention and interest of the marketplace. Ordinary, vanilla and boring "me too" messages are ignored or go unnoticed. Copy (persuasive words that sell) must grab your reader's attention and hold his interest at all times.

8. **It will look like Direct Response Advertising, NOT traditional brand/image advertising.** Emulate only the

ads that sell and move people to action (direct response advertising). Stop emulating any ads that do not sell or rely on hope (traditional advertising that focuses too much on the brand, fancy images and clever slogans).

9. **RESULTS RULE. Period. Nobody's opinion counts, not even yours.** Whenever you stray from the norm of "how we do things around here," and start gaining more success using direct response marketing, you will undoubtedly attract criticism from others: your peers and competitors, your own staff, or even loved ones. You must find the courage to be thick skinned toward criticism. You must stay committed only to results and ignore the rest. Nobody's opinion counts, not even yours. Base your decisions on results and feedback you get from the marketplace, not other people's egos and opinions.

10. **A Commitment To Excellence: Be a Tough-Minded Disciplinarian and take MASSIVE ACTION.** You have to be tough-minded about the money you invest and demand results from anyone that tries to sell you marketing & advertising products or services. Be willing to take massive action and try different ideas, even at the cost of criticism. Jugglers, singers and TikTok "dancers" demand applause. You are a prime mover of society: an entrepreneur, business owner or sales professional. In the end, you write your own ticket. You are the captain of your ship; for you, greatness and achievement are expected.

Examples of Traditional Brand & Image Advertising

Notice how none of these brand ads follow *The 10 No B.S. Rules of Successful Direct Response Marketing.*

They cannot track and measure the success of their marketing because they don't have an offer and a method of response that lets interested prospects know what to do next, where to go, and how to buy. Very vague and unclear.

The big, dumb companies and their even dumber marketing/ad agencies have no idea whether these ads are proving a return on investment or not. My bet is, they're not.

Big companies care more about peer approval. Marketing & ad agencies care more about winning meaningless awards than getting their clients results.

Again, look at their websites and notice how much they love to brag about these awards. Ironically, the marketing agencies that win awards also lose their clients shortly after.

Example of Direct Response Advertising

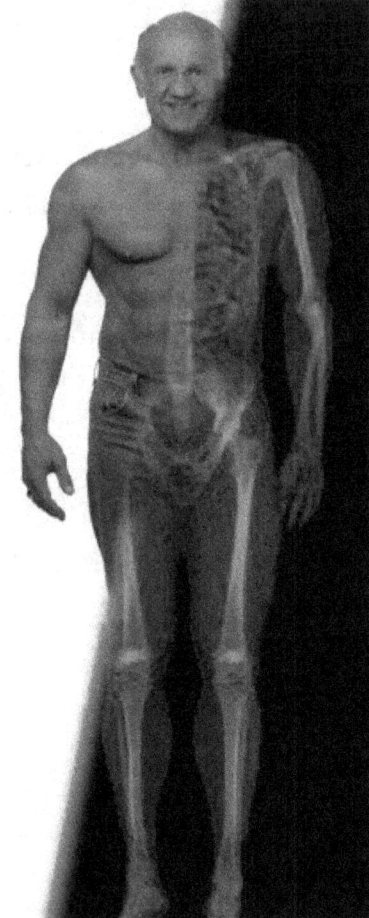

HOW DOES THIS 69-YEAR-OLD DOCTOR HAVE THE BODY OF A 30-YEAR-OLD?

GQ suggests it's the path to *reversing the signs and symptoms of aging.* It's also gotten the attention of *Today, 60 Minutes, Nightline* and *Vogue.*

Find out more about the Cenegenics program, a unique and balanced combination of nutrition, exercise and hormone optimization.

BENEFITS MAY INCLUDE:

Decreased Risk of Age-Related Disease

Improved Muscle Tone

Decreased Body Fat

Increased Energy

Sharper Thinking

Increased Libido

JEFFRY S. LIFE, MD, PhD

Before Cenegenics, Age 64
21% Body Fat
157.6 lbs Lean Muscle Tissue

After Cenegenics, Age 69
10% Body Fat
164.2 lbs Lean Muscle Tissue

**Data compiled by the GE Lunar Prodigy DXA scan
Dr. Life's photo is not enhanced in any way.**

At Cenegenics·, patients are successful business people and professionals. In fact, more than 1,500 of their 15,000 patients worldwide are physicians and their families. **Call today to speak one-on-one with a Cenegenics medical doctor. Strictly confidential, no obligation. Register online to receive the** *GQ* **article and** *The Complete Guide to Healthy Aging.*

Call
866.451.8548

REGISTER ONLINE
www.cenegenics-forb.com

 CENEGENICS

No Insurance or Medicare Accepted.

This successful ad follows our No B.S. direct marketing success rules. It presents a **compelling offer** summarised in the **benefit-driven sales copy.** Even the image is relevant and identifies with the desires of its target prospect.

Notice it doesn't list features, but benefits—**not what the product or service is, but <u>what it can do for you</u>.** It has **clear instructions** on how to respond (call or register online).

Chapter 5: The Marketing Success Triangle

Most business owners and business-building experts don't know what marketing really is.

Most gurus tend to overcomplicate this or try to sound too clever with it. Understand that they're only doing it to confuse you and make you believe what they're doing is new.

None of it is new. Once you understand the PRINCIPLES of marketing, everything else becomes easier.

There are only **3 core building blocks for effective marketing.** That's it.

Here, I present to you the Marketing Success Triangle and the practical, no-fluff definition of what marketing is:

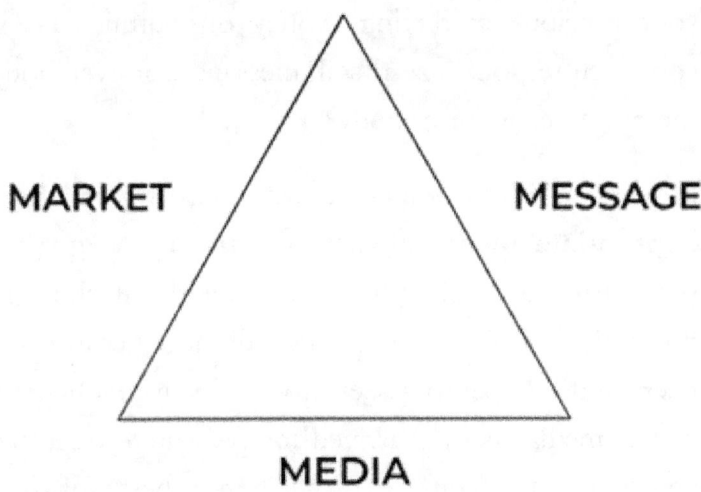

Getting the <u>**RIGHT MESSAGE**</u> to the <u>**RIGHT MARKET**</u> using the <u>**RIGHT MEDIA**</u>—effectively, efficiently and profitably.

This definition is, itself, worth the price you paid for this book a few thousand times over. It dissects questions about your marketing, such as:

- **Is your marketing built around the most powerful, persuasive and compelling message possible?** (Or is your message dull, boring, plain vanilla, me-too-ish, easily ignored, easily compared, forgettable? Or worse, just about an easily replaceable commodity? Or worse still, often about big discounts and lowest price?)

- **Do you know exactly who you're aiming your message at and how you'll put it in front of them?... and how you'll exclude the people it's not for?** (Or are you wasting your precious marketing money on putting out vague, cookie-cutter, one-size-fits-all messages for everybody, and therefore, really for nobody?)

- **Have you identified and are investing in the most appropriate media channels that your target market pays attention to?** (Or are you blindly flushing money down the toilet spending on media just because all your peers and competitors seem to be doing it? Or perhaps a certain media sales rep arrived and pressured you into it? Do you know that different media are best for different businesses with different goals, aiming at different target markets at different times?)

- **Are you accurately tracking and measuring the true NET return on investment from each of your marketing & advertising efforts?** (Or are you guessing? Not really knowing what metrics are truly important, carrying around opinions about vanity metrics that have no positive impact on your bottom line?)

If all this sounds too complex right now, don't worry, you'll gain more clarity and confidence as we continue.

The reason I ask the above questions is to open your eyes to the fact that you need to be a lot better at this than the average marketing team at some ad agency.

When income is small and resources are limited, every good opportunity missed and every bad move made can have major consequences. That's why you must regain ownership and control of your marketing rather than put your trust in marketing agencies.

Realise that the team of "experts" working for marketing/ad agencies tend to be made up of people who've NEVER had to squeeze every drop of profit from every pound or dollar spent.

They came into their jobs from the safe and secure walls of a university lecture hall or seminar room rather than the street.

My goal is to equip you here with the time-tested, fundamental and most powerful marketing principles, strategies and tactics to attract your most ideal prospects using the most appropriate, cost-effective media possible.

So let's dive deeper into the Marketing Success Triangle. **All effective marketing systems are composed of three building blocks: Market, Message, Media.**

- **Market:** Defining, selecting and targeting your highest probability target market—those who are most likely to respond and are willing and able to buy from you.

- **Message:** Carefully crafting a truly compelling message that reaches out to your prospects, grabs them by the eyeballs and demands attention.

- **Media:** Investing in the most relevant and effective combination of media channels used to deliver your message to the right people.

All three are <u>equally</u> important. It's crucial that you don't botch any one of the three. Getting any one of these wrong is a very costly mistake (ask me how I know).

Think of it as a three-legged stool. If you break any one leg, the entire thing is useless. It is a closed triangle. Each feeds the others. Don't be lazy about this. Agonise over each one.

You can render the triangle powerless if you get any one of them wrong. For example, you can craft the most compelling message for the right market, but if you use the wrong media (such as using media they don't pay attention to), then they will never get the chance to even see the message.

Or, you can target the right market using the right media, but if you fail to craft a compelling message, your ad won't grab and hold the attention of your ideal prospects. They won't be able to connect with you. (Are you starting to get this?)

Finally, you can have the right message delivered using the right media, but if you fail to accurately identify the most ideal, highest-probability market to craft your message for, then nobody out there will listen. Worse, you'll only waste your money talking to the wrong prospects.

You must get ALL three sides of the Marketing Triangle right:

Right Message → to the Right Market → Using the Right Media.

That said, a word of CAUTION: The biggest, most expensive mistake most business owners make in marketing today is to *immediately* jump to Media.

They jump straight to media decisions which mainly involve technology and which media platform to use—like SEO, Blogging, Videos, YouTube, Facebook Ads, Google Ads, Email, Instagram, TikTok, etc.

They fail to really think about the specific Market they want to reach, and they fail to craft a truly compelling Message that'll cut through the clutter and resonate with that chosen market.

The sad truth is most business owners have been led to believe that marketing is all about which media platforms they should be in. ***They confuse Media with Marketing.*** It's extremely important that you don't let yourself fall into this trap.

I've just saved you from wasting tens of thousands of your money by falling into the trap of jumping straight to Media without giving careful thought to your Market and your Message.

Again, most business owners CONFUSE Media with Marketing. They have been led to believe that marketing is all about which media platforms they should be on. Thus, when they think about the word "marketing," they automatically think about media and ad platforms.

Wrong. Absolutely, one thousand percent wrong. And anyone who tells you otherwise is a liar and a fraud. Spending money on media just because everybody else is doing so and calling it "marketing" is the fastest way to wind up broke in marketing.

Instead, **whenever you invest in any marketing, you MUST give real, careful thought to all three parts of the Marketing**

Triangle: Market, Message, Media.

Never, ever, ever, ever be fooled into making marketing decisions based on Media alone.

You probably get hundreds of really dumb advice from so-called experts and gurus about which marketing platforms you need to spend money on WITHOUT ever thinking about your Market and/or your Message.

Don't believe them. Don't be taken for a fool. Why do you think they're trying to sell you on the idea that a certain media platform is better than every other media platform? It may be because of the fact that they are SELLING it.

In the next Chapter we'll delve deeper into each of the essential building blocks of your marketing system, starting with your Market—the "WHO" you want to attract to your business.

Chapter 6: Always Start With Your Market (Your WHO)

All great marketing and advertising start with knowing and truly understanding your Target Market—your WHO—your preferred customers, clients or patients.

You must understand your market if you wish to grab and hold their attention amongst all the clutter and noise that they're exposed to every minute of the day.

Long ago, the legendary copywriter Gary Halbert asked his students this question: "If you and I both owned a burger stand and we were in a contest to see who would sell the most burgers, what advantages would you most like to have on your side?"

Most students said they'd like to have the advantage of having superior meat and ingredients. Others said they want to be able to offer the lowest and most affordable prices. Some said they would like to have the best cooks in town and a high-traffic location.

Gary proposed that they could have all the advantages of a great location, superior ingredients, the best prices, the best cooks and the best-looking hamburger stands they could ask for.

All Gary wanted was one advantage and he would whip the pants out of everybody when it comes to selling burgers. The single advantage Gary wanted most was **A STARVING CROWD.**

Your job is to find that starving crowd who can't live without the product, service or solution you provide.

You want to find and target the highest-probability prospects— those who are willing and able to buy, who can be reached affordably, and preferably who already know of you or are likely to trust you.

Once you identify exactly WHO your ideal buyer is—the person you absolutely want to do business with, then you'll be able to craft "magnetic" marketing messages because you'll be able to use words that grab their attention, hold their interest and resonate with their desires. You'll be able to use language they can relate to and talk about what they really want.

What Does Your Ideal Customer, Client or Patient REALLY Want?

Knowing exactly what your ideal customer truly wants is not a simple task. It takes real, deep, careful thought to nail it down.

There's an old sales story about a guy walking into the hardware store and telling the clerk he wants a quarter-inch drill bit. Of course, the mistake most people make is assuming that the actual, physical drill bit was the thing the guy really wanted to buy. Wrong.

The question is WHY does he want the quarter-inch drill bit? What does he REALLY want? He wants a quarter-inch hole. The drill bit is just the mechanism he needs to get it.

If we take it a step further, WHY does he want that hole? What's the underlying problem or desire driving that buying motivation? I assure you, it's not to simply hang a picture.

One of the more likely possibilities is that our prospective buyer craves a lifestyle that presents them as someone with a taste for elegance and culture—which makes their home the envy of friends and family. **For them, it's not just about driving a hole into the wall; it's about <u>Pride</u> and an increased sense of <u>Self-Worth</u>.**

By really understanding your WHO, you went from merely selling the plain, boring deliverable (drill bits) to selling deep, unspoken desires: Pride and Self-Worth.

When you can tailor your marketing to match the deep and unspoken fears and desires of your market, you win.

You'll stand out from the crowd of "me too" messages, you'll attract more attention from your ideal prospects, you'll gain more trust because of how well your message resonates with them, and as a result, significantly increase response from your advertising.

Consider the following two website homepage examples when searching for the keyword "Estate Planning Attorney" on Google.

"Estate Planning Attorney" Example #1

"Estate Planning Attorney" Example #2

Which one would you feel an emotional connection to? Which one would you trust more at first glance?

Example #1 is all about "me, me, me, we, we, we." This is what most big, dumb companies do and what most small businesses try to blindly emulate.

Example #2 is all about the deep worry, fear, and desire of the prospect. **It's about the end result the prospect wants** from the estate planner, which is to make sure everything is taken care of when they're gone.

Market Selectivity: How to Discriminate for Fun and Profit!

Maybe you're already familiar with the idea of "knowing your customer", but I bet **the idea of NOT going after every human with a wallet and a pulse** is probably somewhat of a newer concept for you. Let me illustrate what I mean.

In Aesop's fable *'The Miller, His Son, and the Ass'*, a man and his son walk alongside their donkey as they take it to the marketplace to sell.

They encounter a group of travellers who laugh at them for walking it when they could be riding it. So, the son climbs onto the donkey.

Next, they meet some men who scoff at the son for not

respecting his elderly father and allowing him to ride on the donkey. Although the father didn't mind walking, he trades places with his son.

Later, they stumble upon a woman who criticises the man for making his son walk while he rides. So the boy climbs up and both of them ride until they meet more passersby who say the poor donkey is overloaded.

Of course, the father and son certainly don't want to upset these strangers, so they CARRY the donkey to market.

Two men carrying a donkey attracted a lot of attention, causing the donkey great distress. The poor donkey panics, breaks free of the ropes and falls right into the river.

Million-Dollar Life, Business and Marketing Lesson: When you try to please everyone, you end up pleasing no one (AND you lose your ass).

The *most unproductive and wasteful marketing mistake* **you can make is trying to be all things to all people.** Most businesspeople think everyone is a prospect.

It's hard to please everybody; to be all things to all people. In fact, it's impossible. Everybody is NOT your customer.

The more you focus on trying to go for everybody, the more you neglect the *'somebody'* who will be a better and more profitable customer over the long run.

Most small business owners and entrepreneurs are guilty of "throwing mud against the wall and hoping it sticks" type of marketing—where you throw plain vanilla messages out into the world and hope and pray that somehow the right people will see it and act on it immediately.

Very few business owners ever give this any thought. **Most people's approach to getting new customers is anybody they can get.** You'll never get ahead with this approach.

With direct response marketing, our approach is radically different. Our style is designed to do one very important money-making AND money-saving thing:

To eliminate all the WASTE to the greatest degree possible. Careful Selection and Discrimination of your target market is a must.

Most businesses like to play blind archery. They stumble upon their customers by lucky accident, by launching their messages to everybody, hoping the right people will find it.

Blindfolded, given an unlimited supply of arrows and some luck, you'll hit the target eventually. Arrows are one thing; real, hard-earned money is another. Most small businesses don't have an unlimited supply of cash to play with.

The old theory is that if you broadcast your message enough times in every direction, you are bound to win an audience, and a (tiny) percentage will buy from you.

There's a name for this game. It's called *The Law Of Averages*. It's the same as cold calling a thousand cold prospects and hoping ten will give you an appointment, and one will hopefully buy from you.

If you cold call on a thousand strangers, surely one will bite, right? Even a blind squirrel finds a nut once in a while. However, this is NOT an enjoyable, effective or sustainable approach.

In fact, it's a very costly approach—in time, money and resources. Spending 80-90% of your time and money talking to non-prospects is frankly foolish. This is not the way to play the game.

The best way to market a small business with limited resources is to **be SELECTIVE with whom you want to attract by <u>narrowing</u> your focus to only the people most likely to take advantage of your offer.**

This means you must REPEL and become INVISIBLE to your worst prospects—the bargain hunters, price shoppers, tire-kickers and looky-loos.

Here are the three best ways to narrow your target market and selectively choose your most ideal customer, client or patient:

1. **GEOGRAPHIC:** If you serve a local market, the simplest form of geographic targeting is to focus your marketing within a small, specific area. For example, target only certain postcodes or within a 10-mile radius. Some local businesses don't get any more sophisticated than that. Avoid targeting a big and broad geographic area.

If you're a regional or national advertiser, you can narrow your audience by targeting only the towns, cities and counties where your most ideal prospects reside.

Geographic targeting is the most basic type of target marketing you can do. However, we can be more sophisticated than that and really make every penny we invest in marketing count.

2. **DEMOGRAPHIC:** This is all about having a keen eye to identify the commonalities within your target group of prospects, customers, clients or patients. Look at your customer list and identify all the things they have in common. ***When we find demographic commonalities in a group of customers, we can use those findings to get more of the same kind of customers.***

   Demographic information include: age, gender, income, relationship status, occupation, political views, religious views, etc.

   Demographic selection can be as simple as targeting a preferred age group, or as complex as targeting men living in Southampton, age 35-45, married with two children, and works in construction—which means his health is his wealth. If his body can't perform, his family doesn't eat.

3. **PSYCHOGRAPHIC:** Explains ***why people buy.*** It tells you more about people's hidden desires, deepest fears, attitudes, habits, values and beliefs. To determine this data, start by answering questions like:

111

a) **What keeps them up at night, worrying in pain or frustrated?** If your target market is a small business owner, he may worry about not having enough money for payroll. He worries about having to lay people off because of economic uncertainty.

b) **What is their single, biggest problem** that causes them the most pain and frustration that your product or service can solve?

c) **What do they secretly, privately, desire most?** Put yourself in your customer's shoes and finish the sentence *"If I could just _____, I'd be happy."*

The last question is very important. How do you find out your market's deep, secret and private desires? If you've been in business for a while, think about all the meaningful conversations you've had with your best customers, clients or patients.

You're going to come up with the right answers because you already know them. It helps if you think about your current and past customers who you love to work with, and if possible, you'd love to clone and multiply.

On the other hand, if you're just entering into a specific target market, one of the easiest things you can do to shortcut the research process and still get reliable data is to go to online forums and groups where they hang out.

Start going through posts, comments, threads—and look for pains, problems, and frustrations that you can solve. You'll be able to see what they secretly, privately desire most as it relates to the product or service you offer.

This isn't just about finding out how they feel about what you sell. It's also about discovering how they feel about themselves and what they want for themselves.

If you've walked in their shoes, laughed and cried with them, then you'll begin to understand their real values, beliefs, and motivations for buying.

The "secret" is to tailor your marketing Message to these desires, values, beliefs and motivations. Rather than mainly talking about your product, service or business, you tailor your message to match the emotions and feelings of your prospects.

The WHO Challenge

I challenge you to take a mental picture of your ideal customer. The customer you most enjoy working with. The customer you'd like to have more of, and if possible, clone and multiply.

Put yourself in his or her shoes and write a letter (as your customer) to yourself.

Let's say your ideal customer's name is John. Before John met you, he was struggling for a long time with a problem that you provided a solution for.

Through your marketing and advertising efforts, John

discovered you and came to you asking for help. So you helped him and transformed his life for the better.

Now, if John were to write a "thank-you" letter to you, what would he say? Here's a simple structure to help you get started:

- Dear _____ *[Your Name]*

- Before I met you _____ *[What was going on in my life before I met you]*

- Then I _____ *[What I did differently in my life because I met you]*

- And now my life is _____ *[Describe the after story — the benefits]*

- Thank you for _____ *[What life looks like now — the ultimate transformation]*

- From _____ *[Ideal customer's name]*

Chapter 7: Crafting Your Message (Your WHAT)

By now, you should have a good understanding of your Market (your WHO). Once you've determined who your ideal customer is, you can now confidently talk in their language, and you have the material you need to craft a compelling marketing Message.

When crafting a message, here's what you should think about:

What do you say to your marketplace—to your past, present, and future customers—that is compelling, that cannot be ignored, that must be responded to, that draws them to you like bees to honey?

Do you have a compelling marketing message? Most businesses don't. What typically happens is a person starts a small business and the message is, "We're open for business and looking for new customers — here's a 20% discount, come on in!"

Not bad. It definitely would get lots of responses in 1974, but its pulling power would greatly be reduced in 2024 and beyond. Why? Because there are <u>too many</u> options for the prospective buyer to choose from. In fact, an overwhelming number of options.

This type of "me too" messaging is so commonly used regardless of the market and/or economic conditions.

So if everybody else puts out the same message with the same "XX% discount" offers in front of the same crowd, the effectiveness of the message will wear out, become watered-down, boring, easy to ignore and even easier to forget.

With the ever-growing competition of other similar businesses offering similar types of products or services as you, competing for the same type of customers as you, the more your message needs to be *compelling.* You've got to find a way to separate yourself from the competition and cut through the clutter.

A compelling marketing message is a way of concisely and clearly saying to your chosen market, ***"Here's what I'm all about, and here's why you should choose me."***

The typical business owner hasn't thought about what he's going to communicate to the marketplace about who he is, what he is, and what he's all about that will entice people to want to do business with him.

Instead, he rushes to promote his goods or services by copying what his competitors are doing (but only doing a little bit better) without stopping long enough to consider whether he truly has something worth presenting to the marketplace.

Here's a quick and insightful exercise for you:

Make a list of your competitors who are offering similar solutions to your target market. Now do a quick analysis of these competitors online.

Check their websites, social media pages, online ads etc. Write down each promise, feature, benefit, offer, and statement they make. Have you noticed a trend yet?

On the internet, your competitors are a millisecond's click away. You are all presenting your messages simultaneously to the same target audience. You would think people would give a little more effort in crafting a message that's worth paying attention to.

Despite this obvious and extreme competition for the attention of the marketplace, your quick analysis of marketing messages will expose one revealing fact:

Everybody is saying the SAME thing!

So you need to ask yourself, *"What am I going to say to the marketplace, and why is what I say going to be interesting and appealing to the marketplace?"*

If it's just going to be more of the same as every other business in your category, then forget it. You need to craft a unique and compelling message that helps you stand out from the crowd of me-too competitors.

How to Separate Yourself From The "Me Too" Crowd

In a noisy, cluttered, crowded marketplace, not standing out is the same as being invisible.

To stand out, you must distinguish yourself from the rest of the "me-too" businesses out there, all saying the same things to the same big, broad market.

How do we do that? There are many ways but *The* quantum leap to making your message stand out and separate yourself from the rest of the "me too" crowd is by **crafting a Unique Selling Proposition—a USP.**

The best way to craft a USP is by answering the question almost all your potential customers will be asking themselves:

"Why should I (your prospective customer) choose to do business with you versus any and every other option available to me—including doing nothing?"

Very few businesses give this any thought. Understand that you are not just competing against your competitors, you are also competing against an even more powerful force: *human inertia.*

Most ads have very boring offers and messages; so boring that prospective customers would rather do nothing and watch Netflix all day or mindlessly scroll through their phones rather than finding a solution for whatever ails them.

Naturally, they don't want to give up whatever they're doing just because you happened to show up with an ad offering a big discount or a free consultation.

Presenting a free or low-cost offer does NOT mean there's no risk to it. For the prospect, there's always the risk of their time being wasted—that could be spent on something they know they'll enjoy and are more familiar with.

There must be something that sets you apart. Preferably something that minimises or removes the risks from your prospects and offers them a unique and powerful benefit for doing business with you.

Let's look at an example to illustrate this idea. It demonstrates how a small shop selling a COMMODITY product used a powerful USP to dominate their marketplace.

Over time, this USP was one of the foundations of building the 4.3-billion-dollar business empire it is today.

The commodity business I'm talking about is Domino's Pizza. I put emphasis on the word "commodity" because I want you to realise that if a broke college boy selling one of the most ordinary products in the world can do it, then so can you.

Dominos did not start out as an entrepreneurial empire. Its story began when two young men decided they would put themselves through college by running a small business.

In its early days, they were really struggling to get the business off the ground so one of them cut their losses and bailed out.

The other founder, Tom Monaghan, stayed and stuck it out. He eventually came up with a USP that revolutionised his entire industry and made him a multimillionaire.

Very rapidly, his small business first dominated the local market, then his state, then America, then the rest of the world.

An important side note is the fact that he started out targeting a small local market first, mostly delivering pizza to nearby college campuses—not anybody and everybody in America who can afford a pizza. So he had a clearly defined and narrow target Market.

Anyway, as part of his marketing Message, Tom's USP was: **"Fresh, hot pizza delivered in 30 minutes or less, guaranteed."** If you dissect it, you'll uncover some interesting things.

First, it doesn't claim to be all things to all people. There's no mention of mama's recipe from the old country. There's no mention of a "secret" sauce or special ingredient or a proprietary process. Heck, there's not even a mention of GOOD pizza! (there's truth in advertising after all!)

All it says is they're going to get the pizza in your hands while it's still hot, while it's fresh, and that they guarantee to do that in a specific time period.

It brilliantly incorporated two product benefits:

1. The **Meaningful Specific** of delivery within 30 minutes—not "quick" or "fast"—but precisely in 30 minutes. And...

2. A **Guarantee** that removes a risk the customer doesn't want to take on.

So, what's your USP? It's going to take some careful thought. Somewhere in your business, there's a good answer. If not, you need to make one.

Unfortunately, the first thing most people do when thinking about a USP is to jump to the conclusion that they don't have one—that there's nothing special about their business. In very rare cases, that may be true.

That's when you have to sit down and do some creative thinking and make it into something unique; something different from all your competitors. It wouldn't be too difficult because remember, everybody is saying THE SAME thing.

You make the rules here. Find out a unique and specific advantage you can offer your buyers that no one else can, or no one else is talking about. Let's go through a few ways you can do that.

How to Create Your USP: What Can You Make 'Unique' About You?

Here are three effective ways to help you create your USP:

1. **What specifically do you do that's truly different to your competitors?** For Dominos, this was being there in 30 minutes or less.

   For me, I work with clients as both a marketing consultant and a direct response copywriter. So rather than just writing their marketing materials, I also engage in strategic work to ensure the success of the entire project.

   There are countless consultants and copywriters out there, but there are hardly any single humans who adopt both roles and still perform at the highest level.

2. **Can you niche your target market in a way nobody else can or will?** Joe Weider, co-founder of the International Federation of Bodybuilding (IFBB), built an empire by packaging and marketing weight loss and nutrition products _**exclusively for body builders.**_

   There's nothing different between his products and other similar products sold at general health food stores. But he created a USP by restricting himself to a specific niche, packaging his products and tailoring his marketing to speak only to body builders.

3. **Can you provide a superior guarantee?** The original Domino's USP was guarantee driven. The same with FedEx: "When it absolutely, positively has to be there overnight." FedEx promises fast and reliable delivery service and guarantees that your package will arrive by a certain time.

Take the time to create your own USP. It's one of the most powerful marketing weapons you can ever have for your business.

Follow this simple **3-step USP formula** to help you get started:

We help... *[This group of people]*

Do... *[this benefit/results they want]*

Even if... *[believable worst-case scenario]*

A few examples of a winning USP:

- When you work with me, not only will I help you find the perfect home, but I'll also guarantee that your current home will sell before you take possession of your new one. I'll even double down on that in the unlikely event that your home doesn't sell, I'll buy it myself.

- I show homeowners to save $47,802 of interest expense by changing the way their mortgage is set up, without refinancing their current loan.

- I'm a time management expert who shows executives how to put an extra $4,518 in their pocket every month, by teaching them proven yet little-known productivity and time-saving secrets.

- I show people going through divorce how to avoid an average of $5,678 in unnecessary legal fees, and to get what they want to take out of the marriage without fighting or hassles.

123

- We help maximise retirement clarity—to create, execute and manage effective, efficient, and comprehensive retirement strategies for the affluent professional or entrepreneur.

Compare these USPs to other ordinary businesses around you who are all copying each other, doing "monkey see, monkey do" messaging. Just look around at every business you see and judge their messaging.

You'll see that most people's marketing & advertising look and sound the same, relying on cliches like "the best" or "number one" or "award-winning" or something equally meaningless.

Once you've figured out and carefully crafted your USP, you will almost certainly do better than most of the direct competition around you. Don't miss this. It's The quantum leap for standing out and separating your message from the rest of the me-too crowd.

Now that you've got your USP—which hopefully answers why your prospective buyer should do business with you versus any other option available to do them, you must now…

Make Them An Offer They Can't Refuse

Now, I'm going to take you a step further and power up your messaging with the **creation of an <u>Irresistible Offer</u>**.

The first thing you have to understand is that your offer is NOT your product, service or deliverable.

An Irresistible Offer is: *The "thing" you promote in your marketing and advertising that is a specific combination of features, benefits, bonuses, price, scarcity, guarantee etc. It's something precisely matched to the wants (desires) of the ideal prospect you wish to attract.*

You've got to overwhelm them with value that matters to them. **Most ads are simply a laundry list of features and "me, me, me, we, we, we" speak, which typically includes:**

Company name, logo, image, nonsensical slogan trying to sound smart or funny, bullet list of features/products/services, mentions of how "great" they are, price, phone number, website.

I'm going to be blunt. Your prospective customers don't care, nor do they wish to care about how "great" you say your products are and how valuable you say your brand is.

They do not and will not care unless you first show them you care by understanding and talking about THEIR problems, wants, needs, and desires. Not yours. *Theirs.*

This is the key missing element in most advertising I see: **Benefits.** The benefits of your offer must be specifically and precisely matched to the desires of your ideal prospects.

They are not necessarily coming to you to get your product or service. *They're coming to you for a specific (and often unspoken) set of emotional reasons of their own.*

Your task is to find out what those reasons are—usually their big problems and desires—and position your product or service as the solution. For every problem you solve, explain why it will benefit the customer in every aspect of their lives.

This is different to how most small businesses communicate with their prospects. Most just blurt out a bunch of supposedly great things about their company and a list of facts and features that their prospects either don't care about or can't even make sense of.

One of the best examples of an Irresistible Offer that you can model comes from the hotel and casino business in Las Vegas, where everybody is offered the same thing: a place to lose a lot of money and have fun doing so.

Years ago, one really smart entrepreneur, Bob Stupak, took over the worst and last hotel on the Las Vegas Strip—and turned it into one of the fastest growing hotels now known as *The Strat Hotel, Casino & Skypod*.

At the time, he didn't have bags of money to throw into advertising and marketing, so the conventional ways other bigger Las Vegas hotels promoted themselves were out of his reach.

What did Bob do? He sat down and carefully crafted a very specific Irresistible Offer that he could put in front of his ideal customers and compel them to buy in advance of use.

He filled his rooms selling this irresistible offer.

Here's the offer:

"Give me $396 and I'll give you two nights, three days in my hotel in one of the deluxe suites. There will be a bottle of champagne waiting for you when you arrive. You can have unlimited drinks the entire time you're here whether you're gambling or not.

Even if you're sitting in one of the lounges and enjoying the entertainment, you pay nothing more for your drinks. More importantly, for your $396, I'm going to give you $600 of my dollars to gamble with in my casino."

Notice he didn't bother advertising his hotel as just any other hotel. Instead, **he concentrated his efforts and all his resources on selling that specific irresistible offer to his ideal prospects.**

It also **telegraphs implied benefits** to the reader: a wonderful experience that he/she can brag about to friends and family. In other words, **Increased Enjoyment and Bragging Rights.**

It'll be worth your while to study this offer and ask yourself, *"How can I take this model of an Irresistible Offer and apply it to MY advertising and marketing?*

This is the kind of thinking you need to adopt when crafting your Message. Too many marketers and advertisers come up with an offer that practically forces people to sleep.

Like this: "Special Discount: $35! (normally $105)" or something else that involves zero imagination and barely moves the needle.

127

It's better than nothing, but it is WEAK and any of your competitors can easily copy it.

Frankly, if your offer doesn't cause you to stop, pause, reflect, and think to yourself, "Am I giving away the farm here?" for at least a minute, it's not good enough.

<u>The No B.S. Truth:</u> At its core, marketing is really about motivating people to action, often into doing something they weren't even thinking about doing in the first place.

Today, thousands of advertising and sales messages battle for your prospective buyer's attention every day. This means they'd have to sift through and purposely ignore thousands of messages every day just to pay attention to yours.

If you want to get noticed, you cannot afford to be boring. You *must* stand out.

When it comes to your marketing Message, you stand out by **<u>crafting a winning USP</u>** and by presenting them an "Offer They Can't Refuse"—a truly **<u>Irresistible Offer</u>**.

Chapter 8: Media Is Media Is Media (Your HOW)

So now we've got a great message to present to a great market. Here's the next challenge:

How do we take the Message we so painstakingly crafted and deliver it to a carefully defined and selected Market—<u>via the right MEDIA</u>—in a way that is effective, efficient, and affordable?

As you know, there's practically a never-ending list of media options available today that it's impossible to keep up and be on all of them. The media options available online are especially expanding at a rabbit-breeding pace.

Some appear mighty but then quickly lose momentum or suddenly disappear (like Myspace, Yahoo and Clubhouse) and are replaced by newer, brighter, shinier objects.

When it comes to media choices, what most business owners want to know is: What's the best media? What's the worst? What free media can I use? Is any of it essential?

The truth is there is no simple answer. But the good news is you don't have to be on all of them.

You don't have to be doing random and erratic acts of marketing using media that others have pushed onto you. You don't have to dance on TikTok or spend hours writing and posting free content online hoping that someday, one day, it'll bear fruit.

As said in a previous chapter, one of the biggest mistakes most business owners make when making marketing & advertising decisions is they confuse media with marketing.

This often makes them easy prey and advertising victims for industry vultures peddling media—particularly ONLINE media like Google (SEO & Google Ads), Facebook, websites, videos, email, YouTube, Instagram, TikTok etc.

The No B.S. Truth: Media is Media is Media.

What do I mean by that? **The internet is NOT marketing. It is MEDIA—**<u>online</u>** media. Magazines, radio, TV, any form of direct mail and newspapers are all <u>offline</u> media.**

The cold, harsh truth is this: **Bad marketing—regardless of what media is used to deliver it—IS bad marketing.**

You must really understand that media is NOT marketing. It is only one part of the Marketing Triangle: *Market, Message, Media.*

If you don't have a <u>worthwhile message</u> to present to a <u>carefully selected market</u>, no amount of doing ads or posting free "content marketing" will save you.

It doesn't matter if you use online or offline media if you don't have the other two building blocks of marketing figured out.

Once you understand this critical distinction, you'll forever liberate yourself from the endless (and very costly) cycle of overwhelm, confusion, and participating in random and useless marketing media activities that waste money, time and energy.

Here's the true, workmanlike definition and application of what marketing Media really is:

Media is simply the <u>VEHICLE</u> for which you use to <u>deliver</u> the right Message to the right Market

Media is simply a delivery mechanism. A vehicle used to deliver your message to your intended audience.

That said, there IS a better, more affordable way to decide which media to use to reach your best prospects effectively, efficiently and affordably. It has to do with WHO (the Market) you are trying to reach.

By far, the smartest and most powerful Media strategy of all is this: Go anywhere and everywhere your WHO is paying attention to.

You show up where they show up. You deliver your message in places where they congregate. Wherever their attention goes, it'll be wise for you to show up there.

If they're on Facebook, then show up on Facebook. If they're actively searching for solutions on Google, then show up on Google. If they're dedicated subscribers to a niche magazine that they eagerly wait for every month, then you go there too.

Where Do Your Dream Customers Congregate? — A Russell Brunson Story

If you've ever spent some time on the Internet, you may have heard of Russell Brunson.

He's been taking the "online marketing" space by storm for over a decade, which is a VERY long time in the online world. He must at least be doing something right, and in my opinion, he's a modern-day marketing genius. I don't give out praise willy-nilly.

In one of his books, Russell tells a story of when he was a wrestler in college. Every night, all the student athletes had to spend two hours in study hall to make sure they got their homework done.

In reality, they were all goofing off online and he noticed that he and his friends were all looking at the same website, called *TheMat.com*—a website for wrestlers.

Every member of Russell's college wrestling team was in that study lab for two hours every night, hanging out on TheMat.com and talking about wrestling. But they weren't the only ones hanging out on the website.

Pretty much anyone who was a wrestling fan around the country was also hanging out and having conversations about wrestling on this website.

Given this information, if you were selling a wrestling product or service to student athletes, where would you sell it? One of the best places would be TheMat.com.

You would find the existing congregation of wrestling fans and you would put your message or your bait out in front of them.

In this case, you would already have **the right Market** (student wrestling athletes) and **the right Media** (a website that is all about wrestling). Now, all you would need to have is **the right Message** to grab their attention and begin the process of attracting the right buyers to you.

This example isn't just unique to online. There are congregations online and offline for everything. Online, it could be a website, a Facebook group, or a forum. Offline, it could be a niche magazine, a radio show, a TV program, or a newspaper.

Now, ask yourself this question:

Where are your dream customers congregating—for both online and offline? Make a list.

Because you already know WHO you want to sell to, it's easier to figure out WHERE they are congregating. **Just follow them around.** Go to the same trade shows and events they go to. Read the same books and magazines they read.

Find out the top websites they go to as it relates to your business. What Facebook groups do they participate in? What keywords are they searching for in Google to find information relating to your products and services?

Obviously, if you're a small business and your resources are limited, it's not realistic for you to be on every single media platform there is.

The smart move in the beginning is to only invest in one or two media channels that your ideal prospect pays most attention to—where they hang out the most. Once you've gotten good results from that media, move on to the next, and so on.

There's no such thing as good, bad, best, or worst media. It has everything to do with WHO you are trying to reach. That's why understanding your Market BEFORE spending any money on marketing & advertising is vital.

Before deciding which media channels to use, ask yourself: *"Does my target market pay attention and respond to the media being used?"*

Different types of media channels have their own set of rules and nuances. **As a rule of thumb: If the media can't be used to deliver a direct response message, skip it.**

The truth is you should try to **find ways to use as many different direct response media as you possibly can—a combination of online AND offline.**

Most business owners become lazily dependent on only one or two media sources for getting leads and customers, leaving themselves vulnerable to sudden disruption and entry of more aggressive competition, especially online.

You should integrate online with offline media, so you create the effect of OMNIPRESENCE—showing up almost everywhere your target market is paying attention to.

The leading experts in "online" marketing understand that the internet is nothing more than a collection of marketing and advertising media to be deployed in appropriate situations. It is a big mistake to use and depend on only one media: online.

The one big problem with relying solely on online media is the fact it changes almost every hour of the day. The tech geeks and engineers at Facebook and Google headquarters are paid to play around with and constantly change their algorithms.

They've all conspired to make it difficult for marketers, advertisers and businesses to produce reliable, consistent, long-term results.

Don't get me wrong. Online can be very profitable. I'm not against online media; I'm against being <u>dependent</u> on using only one media.

If your business is dependent on only one media, particularly online media, then you're just one unexpected outage or algorithm change away from not having a business.

And if your ad account or business page gets banned or hacked online, it's over.

You've got to understand that the big online advertising platforms like Facebook and Google do NOT like small businesses.

They don't make their money from small-time advertisers. They make their money from big-budget corporations with unlimited sums of other people's money to play with.

That's why it's ever more important to **use a combination of both online and offline media** to acquire new leads and buyers.

And it's even more important to **collect information about your market**, such as: name, email address, phone number, and physical mailing address.

You need to have their details so you can continue to communicate with them. Because when the big online media companies decide to banish you from their platform, it's game over. It's not a matter of "IF" … it's *"WHEN"*.

Again, don't get it twisted. I'm not against online media. In fact, I'm very much involved in it. BUT it's not the only media I use.

When possible, appropriate and economically affordable, I also use offline media such as direct mail (sales letters, postcards etc.), print, and the phone.

Consequently, this leads me to talk about my favourite offline media: **Direct Mail.**

The Power of Direct Mail

I know, I know. All the fly-by-night marketing experts have pronounced direct mail "dead" since the dawn of the Internet. Unfortunately (for them and those naive enough to believe such nonsense), they're 100% wrong.

I'm here to tell you the idea that direct mail, as an advertising medium, is dead—is complete, and utter B.S. Now I'm not going to harp on about interesting stats and figures to try and convince you. But I will tell you this…

Perhaps the most obvious indication that direct mail still works today is the fact that the online Godzilla, **Google, persists on using direct mail to sell their Google Ads platform to business owners who wouldn't have found them otherwise.**

Google knows that with direct mail, there's significantly less competition, less clutter, less distractions.

Compare this with all your competitors who are using only online creating chaos, confusion and clutter in people's email inboxes, social media news feeds, and competing with thousands of direct and indirect competitors in the Google search listings. But with direct mail, you are instantly granted…

The Power of SHOWING UP <u>ALONE</u>!

In a world where everyone shows up the same way, the long established, familiar brand names have the advantage. **If you are lesser known (but the superior choice), you are starting from a disadvantaged standpoint.**

Here's what I mean. In supermarket shelves, the familiar, over-the-counter brand name items continue to considerably outsell generic versions of the exact same products displayed right next to them on the same shelves—despite the fact these lesser-known/generic brands are selling for 20% to 50% less than the familiar brands.

There are only two sales channels that remove the consumer from competition, chaos, clutter and confusion—and focus him on making a "yes or no" decision after seeing your offer:

1. One is sitting with or across the prospect, selling mano-a-mano, nose-to-nose, toes-to-toes.

2. The other is **a <u>sales letter</u> placed in the prospect's hands, in private, as he sits at his desk and sips on his cup of coffee. With direct mail, you can show up alone and bolt the door behind you when you enter.**

It's the closest you can get to a <u>private, one-to-one sales conversion</u> with your prospective customer without actually being there physically. It gives you the ability to interest, engage and somewhat obligate your prospect for a good amount of time without all the distractions online.

With a real physical envelope and sales letter, you get to have a **PRIVATE conversation** with thousands of properly selected prospects rather than just one.

So contrary to the idea that direct mail is "expensive," it's actually CHEAP when used as part of a more sophisticated, integrated and strategic marketing system.

It's like sending out 2,000 of your best salespeople, carrying your full and best message to the homes and in the hands of your most ideal customers, clients or patients.

And most of the time, these physical letters get to stay inside their homes for weeks or even months, practically reminding them of you every time they see it. It's harder to throw out physical objects, especially if your sales letter delivers a compelling message highly relevant to their problems, wants and desires.

By now you should have a good idea of who your ideal Market is, what your compelling Message will be, and which Media would be most appropriate to deliver your message with.

In the next Chapter, I'll show you how you can position yourself as THE authority in your market, THE expert and THE "guru at the top of the mountain" that your ideal prospects are willing and eager to climb just to get to you.

This is all about putting the power back into your hands and accelerating the Know, Like, and Trust factor.

Chapter 9: POSITIONING—How to Be Seen as *THE* Authority in Your Market

When thinking about finding ways to attract more new customers in the door, business owners often ask the wrong questions. They ask, "How can I find the right customers for my business?"

A better, more purposeful question is: **"How can I POSITION my business the right way so that my ideal customers, clients or patients find me?**

If you want to get REALLY specific, then ask yourself this question: **"How can I get good, qualified prospects to find out about me and seek me out to obtain my expert assistance in solving their problems... where they feel like they are discovering me, instead of me chasing them?"**

See, it's not about you finding customers; it's about engineering ways for customers to find you.

The former is more related to prospecting, which is ugly, grubby, smelly, lots of manual labour work.

The latter requires you to think more about Positioning—how to position yourself and your business so that your ideal prospects find you and seek you out for your expert assistance.

Incidentally, it's good to pursue your prospects in follow-up ONLY once they feel they've discovered you, made the first move toward you, and invited communication from you. But that first move needs to be theirs.

This is not just about getting more customers. This is about getting the *right* customers. It's about attracting customers who respect and value what you do, and are then willing, able and ready to pay for your products or services at the prices you want.

Why is this important? Because **when you go to your prospects for the first time and overtly sell yourself and what you offer, their guard immediately goes up.**

They automatically jump to the conclusion that you're only there to sell them something. That you want something from them. Therefore, sales resistance instantly sets in.

One of the fundamental rules of selling is: **People love to buy, but they hate to be sold.**

If a prospect can immediately tell that they're being hit with a sales message pushing them to leave everything behind and "buy now" or "call now" or "come in now", their resistance goes up.

This is what most small business marketing looks like and it repels a lot of potentially good buyers because they're turned off from the very beginning.

However, when somebody *discovers* you—or at least *feels* like they're seeking you out and discovering you—their guard goes way down. They'll be more receptive to everything you say to them, whether that be in your advertising or when you're on a call or face-to-face meeting with them.

The reason why most small businesses attract poor quality, sceptical, price-driven buyers who are looking for the one magic pill to solve all their problems is because **from the very beginning of the relationship, their positioning is all wrong.**

Poor quality customers often perceive your products or services as a commodity they can access and buy for cheap anytime, anywhere. Thus, the only factor in their mind is "lowest price."

They didn't come in seeking an expert for a real, long-term solution to their problems. They only want someone who can do or provide "the thing" for a low price and be on with it.

These "poor quality" customers often come from poor quality marketing & advertising: poorly selected, poorly attracted, and poorly prepared and conditioned to see you as The authority figure and trusted ally who delivers superior products and services at premium prices.

Sun Tzu once said, "Every battle is won BEFORE it is ever fought." In other words, **what happens BEFORE the selling is more important than the actual selling itself.**

It governs how your client, customer or patient perceives you at the beginning of the relationship, and it governs how they'll perceive you throughout the entirety of your relationship.

This is what Positioning is all about. Winning BEFORE any type of selling, meeting or transaction takes place.

The goal is to **have your marketing do the heavy lifting** for you so that when your prospects come to you, they're already properly selected, properly attracted, and properly prepared and conditioned to perceive you as The trusted authority and ally who is the best choice to help solve their problems.

If you do this well, you'll be able to attract high quality customers who know, like and trust you—and thus, are far more willing to accept and stick with your proposition with minimum sales or price resistance.

You'll spend more time with better-prepared prospects who come to you already predisposed to do business with you over any of your competition or option available to them.

Here are the best ways for positioning yourself, your product/service and your business so that the right prospects discover you and accept you as The expert authority in your category:

Crafting a Unique Selling Proposition (USP)

We've already covered this in *Chapter 7: Crafting Your Message*. Here, I'll briefly touch on it again.

A USP is basically your **positioning statement.** It's your way of saying "Here's what I'm all about and here's why you should choose me."

To stand out from the crowd, you have to offer a unique and distinctive benefit or advantage that your prospect can easily grasp and say to themselves "That's FOR ME!"

You must find something unique (or can be made unique to you) that tells your prospects you're not like everyone else.

Because if you're doing and saying the same things as everybody else, you'll be perceived as just one of the same choices that are out there. In other words, just another commodity. Easily compared, easily replaced, and can easily be beat down on price.

So when you create your USP, the more clearly you can telegraph why you're the better choice to solve their specific problem, the more likely you will be chosen.

You must have an answer to the following USP question:

"Why should I, your prospective buyer, choose to do business with you versus any and every other option available to me—including doing nothing?"

Why is it so important that you have a well-crafted answer to this question? Because in today's fast-paced world, people are faced with so many choices in their day-to-day lives that it often creates a lot of paralysis.

Too many options. Too much to think about. You know what's easier? If I just do nothing.

So you're not only going up against your direct and indirect competitors, but you're also going up against human inertia, sloth, laziness—and mostly, fear of making the wrong decision and being judged and criticised by others as a result.

When faced with too many of the same "me too" options, humans find it easier to just do nothing. That's how most people are wired.

So you have to stand out and really turn your back from the "mee-too-ism" of your industry. If you want to succeed, you can't look, sound or smell like everyone else. It's too dangerous.

Writing: You Must Publish... or Perish

Everyone who has manufactured authority status for themselves have this in common:

They all write (or hire a writer) and publish on all the appropriate media channels they can possibly publish their message on.

Publishing articles, guides, books, special reports and

newsletters accelerates the "Know, Like, and Trust" factor.

There is no more essential tool of authority than authorship. It's in the word: **Author-ity.** And when it comes to authority positioning, nothing beats an actual, physical book.

If you're serving a broader (or global) market, a digital book is also good enough. Depending on your resources and your market, you can choose whether you want to write a physical or digital book. Best if you have both.

Regardless, if you want authority status, you need to have a book. It will be **your primary weapon for setting you apart from your competitors and position you as more than just another vendor of goods or services.**

Take this book for example. It's about how to create a system to attract ideal prospects consistently and predictably—with all the meat—and minus all the fluff other book authors tend to add on.

I wrote it for small business owners, entrepreneurs and sales professionals who want the WHAT, the WHY, and the HOW-TO information in order to help them implement fast.

Essentially, you can do the same thing. It doesn't have to be 200+ pages. You can write a condensed 50–80-page book focusing on a very narrow subject around a specific problem you can solve for your target market.

It's going to be designed to take them through your step-by-step process of how to solve their problem and why they should be working with you.

So while you're giving them the keys to help solve their problem on their own, you're also establishing trust, authority, credibility and expertise.

Chances are, **a certain percentage of people who get your book will come to the conclusion that they don't have enough time, knowledge, resources or expertise to do it themselves, so they'll come to you for help.**

You can choose to charge a small price for it or simply give it away free. If you're thinking of giving it away for free as a lead generation magnet, you should only do so if you're confident you're giving it away to carefully selected prospects—those who fit the description of your ideal customer, client or patient.

Otherwise you'll attract a lot of flaky, poor-quality leads… and waste a ton of time, money and resources in the process.

The biggest benefit of publishing a book (or a definitive guide or special report) is that when it comes to marketing, it positions you in a way that nothing else can:

You are no longer selling or perceived as selling. Instead, you're providing valuable information that can help your prospect solve their problem.

The prospect's perception of you has shifted from "he's just trying to sell me his products or services" to "this guy must be an expert in solving my specific problem. He wrote the book on it!"

Society in general holds books and authors in high esteem. Most people don't throw books away. Our culture frowns upon destroying books.

Even if you're not interested in reading a book, you may place it near your desk, on your coffee table, beside your bed, or even give it away to a friend or a local bookstore. But you will never destroy or toss one away.

This is the same with your prospects. Even if they don't read your book, they'll place it somewhere they can see.

Every time they feel the particular pain you help solve, they'll be reminded about your book which tells them exactly how to solve it, thereby demonstrating you are the expert authority they should look for if they ever want more help.

Advanced Tactic: When you advertise, you can choose to promote your book (or guide, special report, masterclass etc.) rather than your business, products or services.

If you look through any directory, online or offline, you'll find dozens of listings for your category of business. What could possibly compel a busy person to choose your business, products, or services over another?

My mentor, Dan Kennedy, developed a creative solution to this problem. Years ago, he consulted with Dr. Robert Kotler, a cosmetic surgeon in Beverly Hills, California, who wrote a book, cleverly titled *The Consumer's Guide to Cosmetic Surgery.*

While other surgeons spent outrageous amounts of money to advertise their practice in high-end Beverly Hills magazines, Dr. Kotler immediately stood out amongst the clutter of "me too" surgeons who were all showing up in the same media (magazines) and were all asking the reader to "book a consultation now."

Instead, Dr. Kotler stood out from the crowd by advertising his book rather than directly advertising his practice and asking people to book a consultation.

In addition to getting quality leads who were interested in learning more about getting cosmetic surgery, Dr. Kotler also **elevated his status as _The_ expert authority**, giving more opportunities for prospective patients to respond and seek him out for advice.

The book also made him into somewhat of a local celebrity, getting invited to local talk shows and to do lectures.

You can do the same thing for your business. It's worth noting that if this works even in an extremely competitive, expensive and highly regulated environment such as selling cosmetic surgery in Beverly Hills, then you can surely find a way to make it work for your business.

Manufacture Authority by "Speaking To Sell"

Being at the front of the room speaking to your ideal prospects is a very effective way to be seen as an expert and have eager prospects coming to you for further assistance.

It's also efficient because **instead of spending your time selling one-to-one, you're selling one-to-many.**

Go online and search for Associations or Clubs in your city and nearby areas. There are business groups, civic groups and special interest groups. Most have monthly meetings and they're always looking for speakers with specialised knowledge.

Don't just speak at any group that would have you. Again, it's important to do your research. You should only contact local groups and chapters of national associations where you believe a good number of your ideal prospects are gathered.

It's easier now than ever to get yourself booked to speak. Most communities have several clubs, networking groups, meetup events, chambers of commerce and many other local associations.

Most of these people gather for breakfasts, luncheons, dinners and meetings for which speakers with interesting topics are needed. The online equivalent of these are podcasts.

Make a list of podcast hosts that your ideal audience watches and listens to. They're also always looking to interview an expert with thought-provoking topics their audience would be interested in.

Now, the biggest concern about public speaking is the fact that more people are afraid of it than of just about anything else.

However, the biggest advantage is also the fact that IF you (or someone in your team) will do it capably and confidently, *it automatically gives you a certain level of authority.*

The person on stage, microphone in hand, is automatically seen as the expert simply by being the person on stage, microphone in hand.

So if you have a well-crafted selling presentation that makes the audience aware of their problem, demonstrates your expertise and provides them with effective solutions, then you are starting from a very good place.

And if you are put at the front of the room by an organisation, company, or host who already has authority with the audience, then as they pass the microphone to you, they also pass their influence and authority over to you—**giving you instant trust and authority _by association_.**

Huge Time-Saver: **You can also turn a great speech into a book.** Dr. Maxwell Maltz's book, *Psycho-Cybernetics*, was formed using material from his lectures about the self-image. Dale Carnegie's book *How to Win Friends and Influence People* came from his classes about public speaking.

Get Invited In and Welcomed as The Trusted Authority via Lead Generation Advertising

Another way to position yourself and your business as The authority in your field is to **switch from all other forms of advertising** (e.g. overtly advertising your business, product, service, deliverables) **to Lead Generation Advertising.**

What is Lead Generation Advertising? **Its underlying premise is to engineer a predictable process where you are sought out, invited in, and welcomed as an expert advisor.**

In the book *The 48 Laws of Power*, author Robert Greene teaches that one of the keys to power is in making others come to you and using bait if necessary. He says:

"When you force the other person to act, you are the one in control. It is always better to make your opponent come to you, abandoning his own plans in the process. Lure him with fabulous gains—then attack. You hold the cards."

Now, don't take the quote too literally. Use common sense and adapt it to your specific situation. Your prospect is obviously not your opponent, but the idea is powerful if applied in marketing.

It is my firm belief that the concept of attracting and getting the right people to raise their hand and invite you in for further communication about what you offer is far more powerful than any form of pushing, chasing, hunting, begging or pursuing.

In the next Chapter, we're going to delve deeper into what lead generation advertising & marketing is, why it's so important, and how you can apply it to attract prospects who desperately want and need what you're selling.

"This Sounds Like An Awful Lot Of Work"

That's because it IS. And it's most definitely a lot of work <u>upfront</u>. That's the key.

We do a lot of heavy lifting from the very beginning. But once we've done the work, we can then integrate it into our marketing SYSTEM, which will work for us even when we're away—like a well-oiled, cash-generating machine that never sleeps.

Once we've published our books, special reports, guides, 'how-to' videos, etc., then we can use them over and over and over again in our marketing. **Our goal is to get as close to "set it and forget it" as we possibly can.**

With my methods, the work is front-end loaded. This means you have to do a lot of work in the beginning to assemble your tools, engineer your system and get it functional, up and running.

Once done, it does a lot of the work for you with very little manual labour required on your part.

You'll be able to sleep soundly knowing that your marketing system is working 24/7, then wake up the next day with sales made or booked solid with appointments from highly qualified prospects and ready buyers.

Compare this with the other lazier, "easier" approach of just overtly selling—pushing your goods or services down people's throats and showing up in the marketplace with the typical "buy now" and "book a call now" type of offers.

Not the best way to stand out and be perceived as the expert authority. With the overt salesy approach, you're perceived as just another salesperson, and the marketplace will treat you as such.

Let me put it this way: say you were a 52-year-old construction worker suffering from severe, chronic back pain that's stopping you from lifting heavy objects.

Wouldn't you rather seek out and trust the expert chiropractor who wrote the book on *"6 Easy Ways to Relieve Back Pain For Construction Workers Aged 50 And Above"* than the salesy general chiropractor who treats anyone and everyone, and is always pushing you to leave all your plans behind and risk coming to his clinic just because they're having a "special discount" for your first exam/consultation?

And if you get follow-up material or a call from the assistant of the expert who wrote the book on your nagging back pain, wouldn't you be more likely to pay attention to it than a follow-up from a random salesperson just calling to try and book you in for an appointment?

And when you do finally seek out the expert chiropractor to

diagnose and prescribe the solution to your back pain, you're far less likely to resist that treatment or balk at the price.

You'd be more open to the expert chiropractor's advice and you're more likely to stick with their treatment plan.

So, ask yourself, do you want to keep getting sceptical, flaky, price-driven, "would be" customers, clients or patients who don't see the value in your expertise?

Or do you want highly qualified, committed customers, clients or patients who see you as a trusted ally, as The expert advisor that can help transform the quality of their lives?

The No B.S. Truth: How you are perceived from the very BEGINNING of the relationship determines how you'll be perceived THROUGHOUT the entire relationship.

Take your pick. A welcomed expert advisor OR an annoying salesperson? This is more than a choice of business strategies. This is a *lifestyle choice.*

Chapter 10: How To Use "Lead Generation Advertising" To Attract Highly Qualified Prospects

Lead Generation is the process that transforms you into being: **Always the "Welcome Guest", Never the "Annoying Pest."** Here's what I mean...

How do you feel when a dear friend whom you haven't seen in years suddenly shows up at your door? Pretty excited, right? Now compare that to how you feel when a stranger shows up at your door and tries to sell you something.

You're most likely going to welcome the friend with open arms but take on the stranger with your guard all the way up.

In short, the friend is a welcome guest, and the stranger is seen as an annoying pest. The friend brings value into your life whereas you see the random stranger/pest as someone trying to interrupt you and get something from you.

Most small business marketing and advertising is like the annoying pest.

They barge into the person's home, interrupt their family dinner, and try to get them to drop their current and future plans to "book an appointment now" (or "buy now"). They try to sell without first building trust. In the absence of trust, you are seen as just another vendor or seller.

The problem with outright selling the very first time you meet someone is the fact that even if the person is suffering from the problems you solve, they still don't know you, still don't like you, and still don't trust you.

Your prospects are sceptical because they've most likely tried other remedies and solutions in the past but have been let down more times than they'd like to remember.

Knowing this, it's important to understand that the vast majority of the time that you try to communicate with your past, future, or current customers, you are categorised as a pest, not as the most welcome guest.

But if you change that, you change everything. Everything else suddenly gets easier if you become a "Welcome Guest." And **it all starts with switching from all other forms of advertising to LEAD GENERATION Advertising.**

The goal of Lead Generation is to get the qualified

prospect to raise his hand and identify himself as 'interested' in learning more about what you offer.

The best way to do this is through direct response advertising: where you specifically ask the prospect to take action and respond to your ad in order to get more information about the offer.

In other words, you get your ideal prospect to step out of the crowd, raise their hands, and identify themselves as qualified and interested in your message. You do this with an ad, a sales letter, a postcard, an email, or other means.

Those interested in your ad will step forward and ask to be provided with more information in exchange for their contact information. **Those who respond to your ad are now what we call "leads."** Our goal is to build a <u>bank</u> of leads.

Leads aren't something you take out of a directory and send cold emails to. Those aren't leads. What I define as **a real "Lead" is an ideal prospect who has expressed interest in your offer by giving you their contact details and inviting you in for further communication about the topic.**

Building a bank of leads is important because now you have a list of your target prospects you can confidently and continually send relevant marketing communications to. They have stepped out of the crowd and identified themselves as interested in receiving more information from you.

Here's the big reason why this is important:

The No B.S. Truth: Most people you reach with your advertising & marketing are NOT ready to book a consultation or buy right now.

By only providing one way to respond (buy now or book an appointment now), you leave out all the prospects who are suffering from the problem you solve BUT just aren't yet ready to commit right now—for various reasons.

One of the biggest reasons is the fact they don't know, like, or trust you yet. Another is the fact that asking a stranger to buy from you (or commit a time with you) the very first time they meet you places a huge time and financial risk on them. Thus, a big no-no.

However, through lead generation advertising—offering a "Lead Generation Magnet" rather than directly selling or asking for the consultation—you're able to build a bank of leads: people who have raised their hands and identified themselves as "interested" in what you're selling.

This enables you to continuously follow-up and communicate with them until they're ready to actively seek you out for your expertise.

Very important concept. Yet hardly any small business owner or service provider truly grasps its power to reinvent and transform any type of business, in any category, forever.

Also, by changing FROM traditional advertising and "buy now" advertising TO Lead Generation Advertising, **your prospects feel**

like they are "discovering" you instead of feeling like they're being hunted, chased, and pestered by you.

This simple change in your new-customer acquisition process greatly affects how they perceive you (salesman or expert?) and their willingness to follow your advice.

So you use lead generation advertising to ferret out the most likely prospects and get them to start the process of raising their hands, stepping forward and coming to you... instead of you chasing them, trying to convince and justify along the way.

Done properly, you are making the prospect <u>feel in control</u> of the whole buying process because they're the ones seeking you out and inviting you in as a Welcome Guest.

You're letting them take the desired action when THEY are ready, without pressure of being "sold."

How Lead Generation Advertising *Actually* Works

The way you write lead generation ads is **like opening or closing a faucet to control water flow. You have to make decisions about how much flow you want.**

If you make your lead generation ad as appealing as humanly possible and present it to a large number of people, you're essentially opening the faucet as far as you can to get as much water as you can.

Normally, the large, national direct response companies do this because they have an in-house telemarketing or sales team who needs to talk to every lead they can get.

They don't typically care about the quality of the lead because their salespeople are good enough to turn a "C-Grade" lead into an "A-Grade" lead.

Most likely, you don't have a business with a room full of really good salespeople sitting around waiting for leads to talk to. In this situation, you're better off tightening the faucet WAY DOWN.

This means **you're willing to spend MORE to get a high-quality lead, rather than spend a ton of money getting a truckload of low-quality leads** (which you'd then still have to spend more time and money filtering the good ones from the bad).

Incidentally, this is why **it's a mistake to measure the effectiveness of your advertising in terms of "Cost Per Lead" (CPL).**

You'll see a lot of pretend experts today trying to convince you that a low cost per lead is a good thing. Maybe it is. Maybe it isn't.

When it's all said and done, it's all about the ROI. **The only true metric that counts is the Return On Investment.**

So although "low" cost per lead can help indicate the success or failure of a campaign, at the end of the day, **it's all about the quality of that lead and whether that lead turns into a valuable** and profitable customer, client or patient who PAY, STAY, and REFER.

ROI is the only true metric that matters. Don't let techno babbling Internet freaks tell you otherwise.

If an "expensive" lead turns into a long-term customer who then stays with you for 10 straight years and refers their friends and family to you, how much is that lead really worth?

It doesn't matter if the cost of acquiring that really good lead is £500. Let's say the lead turns into a first-time buyer and spends £300 with you. The dumb businessperson or so-called expert might say that's a £200 loss.

Now what if that new customer comes back and spends another £300. Now he's worth £600. In total, he spends £600 per year over 6 years. Money math says that the £500 lead is actually worth at least £3,600 to you over the course of the business relationship.

And what if they referred at least one of their friends and family to you every year for the next five years (i.e. you're getting a new customer for free). Now what is that lead REALLY worth?

If the average good customer is worth £3,600 to you in lifetime value, and he brings 5 more great customers just like him for FREE (through referrals), that's a total value of £18,000 in referrals alone.

In short, that supposedly "high cost" £500 lead is actually worth £3,600 + £18,000 = **£21,600 over the course of the entire business relationship.** That is how you should see a good quality lead from a good quality media source.

Now, that "high cost" per lead may not be so high after all. As a matter of fact, it's more like a bargain. Compare that to getting a bunch of broke, price-driven leads acquired for the sake of getting a "low" cost per lead. Is that really an achievement? No.

The lesson is **you shouldn't solely base your media choices and marketing investments based on how "low" you can pay for a lead.**

So if doing direct mail costs you £500 to get a lead but that lead becomes a very long-term and profitable customer that's worth over £21,000 over the course of your business relationship, the smart businessperson would find a way to PAY for that lead even if there are other "low cost" online media options.

Bottom line is you should pay for EVERY media source you can possibly afford to acquire leads and buyers. As long as the numbers show that your media source attracts quality leads who end up being profitable buyers for you, you should continue using it.

In the end, **it's all about their Return on Investment (ROI) over the course of the entire business relationship (Customer Lifetime Value).**

That means you need to track how much return you're getting from that lead for as long as they're doing business with you.

Do NOT judge the value of your leads based on the first transaction only. That's the <u>wrong number</u>. Business decisions based on wrong numbers can lead to devastating consequences.

Smart marketers and business owners would much rather spend MORE to acquire better, higher value leads that turn into customers who pay, stay, and refer... rather than spend "less" to acquire low cost, low-quality leads that don't translate into profits or ROI.

Most business owners are cheap about this. That's probably why they attract the same type of customers to their business. Price-shoppers, bargain hunters, tire kickers. I.e. Cheapskates.

How to Write Pro-Level Lead Generation Ads

A lead generation ad should work like a "personals" ad—a form of advertising in America in which a person seeks to find another person for friendship, romance, marriage or sexual activity.

In the UK, it was commonly known as an advert in the "lonely hearts" column—a newspaper or magazine column containing ads from readers looking for a partner or lover.

<u>Lead Generation Ads are written to do two important things:</u>

1. **To <u>attract responses</u> from carefully described people (your WHO).**

2. **To <u>discourage responses</u> from those who do not meet the desired qualifications (tightening the faucet down).**

164

This approach works for most products, services, and businesses. Here's an example of a pro-level lead generation ad for a financial advisor that accomplishes these two things:

WARNING FOR MARRIED OWNERS OF BUSINESSES, EXECUTIVES, AND ENTREPRENEURS WITH TAXABLE INCOMES OVER £200,000 PER YEAR.

YOU are the government's #1 target. Your net, combined tax load could be as much as DOUBLE in the next 12 months. Your pension fund or retirement savings is at new risk. Do you know the TRUTH about the government's plans for your hard-earned money?

MY FREE REPORT: "FINANCIAL ALERT!" reveals the details in plain English... CALL: a free recording message at 00000-000-000 or request your Report online at www.taxalert.com.

If you study this ad carefully, you'll see that it *telegraphs* **to a certain, carefully defined group of people** and *excludes* **those that do not meet the requirements.** Also notice that the ad does NOT talk about the planner, products, services or the company

The person responding to this ad meets a certain demographic and mindset profile. At this point, the person responding feels he is taking the first step to solving his financial-related frustrations and <u>discovering</u> the trusted expert who can help.

What happens next? When the prospect who meets the desired criteria responds, the financial planner sends the report with a package of relevant and related promotional materials.

These marketing materials are designed to establish the financial planner in the right role with the right positioning, which is: Trusted Advisor... Expert Authority... Always the Welcome Guest, Never the Annoying Pest.

Unfortunately, most businesspeople would jump to the misguided conclusion that this does not apply to THEIR business.

The common self-imposed limitation is "Yes, this works for XYZ company, but MY business is different."

If you're not a financial planner, it doesn't matter. I used a lead generation ad by a financial planner just as an example, but the goal is the same for EVERY business who's looking to have their ideal prospects step out of the crowd and come to them for help.

The goal of your lead generation ad is not to overtly sell your products or services.

The goal of lead generation advertising is simply to **get our ideal prospect to raise their hand and identify themselves as having interest in solving the problem that you solve.**

If they respond to your lead generation ad, they're inviting further communication from you, making you a "Welcome Guest."

This allows you to further market to them (via follow-up) until they are ready to take the next step—to schedule an appointment or buy now.

Again, to write effective lead generation ads, you must:

1. Know WHO you **want** to respond. And...

2. Know WHO you **don't want** to respond.

Once you figure out the ideal prospect you want to respond, you now need to write a compelling message that calls out your ideal prospect and repels the people you don't want.

I highly recommend you study the lead generation ad example above and model it. See how it compares to your current ads.

How to Craft The Right Lead Generation Magnet To Attract Your Ideal Customers

To make lead generation advertising work for your business, you need a **Lead Generation Magnet (LGM).** An LGM is the **"widget" you offer as either a free or low-priced incentive for response.**

The best LGMs are **information about a specific subject of prime interest to your target prospect** (not anyone and everyone with a wallet and a pulse). Informational LGMs tend to be the most effective at stimulating response for the simple fact that:

When someone becomes aware they have a problem and they want to solve it, what they're typically looking for is information to help them make the right decision.

When you can provide that information for them; when you can show them that you understand their specific problem and that you may have the solution they've been looking for, then you position yourself as the trusted authority in solving that problem.

Their perception of you immediately changes from "salesperson trying to sell me something" to "expert I can trust and who might be able to help me with this."

This instantly separates you from everybody else who is overtly trying to sell them on heavily discounted products and services. It also helps accelerate that Know, Like, and Trust factor.

For example, imagine you were an **estate agent** targeting 65-year-old couples interested in buying a second home by the seaside to retire in. You could offer a free report as your LGM, titled '*10 Best Seaside Towns to Retire To In The UK.*

In this report, you promise to reveal ten of the most beautiful beachfront retirement communities in the UK that have seen INCREASES IN HOME VALUE. You'll also include descriptions of these communities, pictures of the rooms and amenities, and the pros and cons of each area.

Another example, if you were a **chiropractor**, you could offer a free report as your LGM, titled '*5 Ways To Have A Pain-Free Back In 6 Weeks.*'

Obviously, one of the five ways would involve coming into the clinic for an exam and possibly, treatment. However, the other four ways would be useful things your prospect can do on their own to relieve back pain.

Those who are convinced and trust that you can help them faster, safer and better than they can help themselves, will come to you.

You can also continue to follow-up with relevant marketing messages and offers to those who have shown interest (became leads) but have *not yet* taken the next step (made their first purchase or booked an appointment).

You have already invested money to acquire these leads, now you need to engage in continuous and relevant follow-up marketing in order to stay in front of the competition and on top of your prospects' minds.

Your LGM does not always have to be a free report. If you're comfortable on camera, you can create a "how to" video series demonstrating your expertise. Or you can create a webinar to help educate your target market about their problem.

Here are a few important tips when creating your LGM:

1. **Avoid "Me, Me, Me, We, We, We" Speak.** Some lead generation magnets talk too much about themselves, their staff, their price, their products or services—yet never enough about the prospect.

   The prospect will not care about you unless you first show you care about him. And what he really cares most about are the wonderful things that will happen to him as a result of doing business with you.

   Translate every feature listed in your LGM into a real,

transformative benefit for the customer. Use the data you gathered about your Market (your WHO) and talk to them in their language—about their problems, how you can solve them, and how amazing their lives would be once you've helped them.

2. **Don't Over-Educate. You want to inform and impress, but not tell them everything you know.** It will only overwhelm and confuse them.

   Tell people what to do and give them only the basic "how to do it" in simple language they can understand (not every little nuance of how to do it). Your prospects don't need to know every little thing that's involved in the process. It'll only confuse them. Confused prospects don't buy.

   They just need to understand the concepts and believe you can help them move away from pain or move towards gain. One of the best responses you can get to your LGM is "Can you help me?"

3. **Don't Forget The Call-To-Action (CTA).** If you don't have a call to action enticing them to take the next step, you've wasted your time and money. You must tell your prospect exactly what you want them to do next and what will happen when he does.

   It's helpful to offer an incentive for taking that action, such as a bonus gift and/or a new-customer discount.

   Your CTA could be a number of things. You could send them to a website for additional information and resources.

You could invite them to visit your online store and buy now. You could invite them to a call or in-person meeting.

Why Lead Generation Advertising Is SO Important?

Let's quickly recap what we've covered so far. WHAT is the job of lead generation advertising and WHY is it so important to switch from all other forms of advertising to lead generation?

First, to elicit response from your preferred customer and repel those you don't want to respond. Why? Because we don't want to waste any money on people who aren't going to be good customers anyway e.g. price-shoppers, tire-kickers, bargain hunters, and those who don't respect or value your goods or services.

Second, to reinforce and strengthen the prospect's unhappiness with the current circumstances and problems he has, that you are the solution to.

Third is Positioning. To establish both your expertise and empathy. By positioning yourself as an expert authority rather than just a salesperson or vendor, the prospect sees the value in what you provide and is predisposed to accept your propositions and recommendations favourably.

Fourth, NOT to make the quick sale, but to set up the sale and foundations for a profitable, long term, trust-based relationship. The relationship you cultivate with your customers, clients or patients is the number one asset you have in business. If you have buyers who are eager to choose you over anybody else in your field, you'll thrive even during the darkest of times.

Last but definitely not the least, to build a bank of leads that can be nurtured and developed through follow-up until they're ready to buy. If you have a bank of leads consistently coming through the pipeline, you have a bank of dependable future money.

If you don't have that, you only have the constant hope AND worry of "who's gonna come in today?"—As you know, this type of thinking does many bad things.

It causes you to reluctantly take on poor quality customers, clients or patients you shouldn't take and don't want to deal with. Not only does this cause anxiety and desperation, but it also causes tremendous fear, hatred and frustration because you don't know when and where your next customer is coming from.

The solution is to devise a predictable SYSTEM that will consistently generate a bank of qualified leads who are on the verge of buying or will be ready to buy soon.

If you don't have this, you choose to rely on the guy who needs your goods or services today but is only looking for the cheapest option available. The only question for this type of prospect is "Who has the lowest price?"

Chapter 11: Lead Development & Conversion System—How To Turn Leads Into Booked Appointments Or First-Time Buyers

Once you've gotten your ideal prospect to step out of the crowd, raise his hand and express interest from your lead generation offer, it's time to begin the Lead Development and Conversion process.

Your Lead Development & Conversion System has one goal: **to turn qualified leads into paying customers, clients or patients.**

This is done by sending relevant follow-up messages to turn the leads you've acquired from a "merely interested" prospect to a fully engaged, first-time customer.

Here are the components of your Lead Development & Conversion System to turn leads into buyers:

1. **Multi-Step Campaign**

2. **Additional Content**

3. **Shock & Awe Package**

4. **Consultation Offer or Buy Now Offer**

The different components can be mixed and matched and sequenced in different ways.

This will depend on a number of things, including your unique business operations, the attitudes and behaviours of the marketplace, your staff/employees, your typical sales cycle, your numbers, resources, and other factors unique to you, your business and your industry must come into consideration.

In other words, it's up to YOU to decide exactly how to configure your System for developing and converting leads into buyers.

As a guide, you should use a combination of the components above as it suits your goals and resources. Whatever the case, you must have a predictable SYSTEM for turning those leads into appointments or buyers.

That means **you must have marketing materials, assets and processes in place to follow up with your leads.** Far too many marketers and business owners totally drop the ball when it comes to following up with leads who've clearly expressed interest in what they have to offer.

You've paid good money for effective lead generation

advertising, paid tools, software, physical location, energy, your team, and more—yet you're willing to watch all that go down the drain by failing to follow up with good, high-probability leads.

When you fail to follow up on leads, you must understand that you not only pay for the customers you get, but you also pay a price for *every* website visit, *every* call, *every* walk-in, *every* appointment etc.

Doing nothing with one lead is bad business.

I grew up poor. I came from a financially struggling, third world, immigrant background. My parents came to the U.K. with barely a penny to their name.

Early in life, I remember seeing 12-year-old kids roaming the streets of a busy airport at three in the morning, scraping through dirty, stinky bins just to get their hands on cold, mushy leftovers thrown away by tourists.

That image stuck with me. Since then, I have not been and will never be fond of letting any opportunity go to waste.

Doing nothing with each new opportunity to get a customer is like flushing money down the toilet. Picture this:

If you spend £1,000.00 on an ad campaign and get 50 phone calls, you paid £20.00 for each call. If you're going to waste one, you may as well get a nice, crisp £20.00 note, tear it in pieces, let the pieces flutter into the toilet and flush.

Watch it go away. If you're doing nothing with 30 of those 50 calls, stand there and do this task 30 times. How does it feel? Remember this feeling every time you fail to follow up on a lead or customer.

By deploying an effective System for developing and converting leads, you instantly set yourself up for greater business success because you are staying "top of mind" by sending frequent and relevant communications that your prospects are interested in.

It'll only be a matter of time before your prospect will have to make the inevitable "no brainer" decision of choosing you over any and every other option available to them.

Let's talk about a few ways to do just that and dive deeper into each of the main components of your Lead Development & Conversion System.

The Magic of The Multi-Step Campaign

Most small business marketing is unsophisticated, random and erratic. They do what I call One-Shot Marketing: sending out a single piece of promotional item to a big, broad and cold audience with the sole purpose of turning them into customers right now.

Effective marketing does not work that way. It's extremely rare to get a good return on investment if you send out only one piece of marketing only ONCE to a big, broad market.

You can't expect strangers to buy now or schedule a call with you at the very first message they receive from you.

Yet that's how most small businesses do marketing. They send out leaflets, postcards and flyers once a quarter, hoping you would call or buy right now.

Reality is, the vast majority of people you present your advertising and marketing to will NOT be ready to buy or commit to anything right now. This process takes time, frequency, consistency, and concentrated, purposeful effort.

How often have you immediately purchased from someone you just met? Probably not very often—only when you really, really needed it; if you were desperate for it, had no other choice, or it was an emergency.

Other than those situations, for the most part, if the commitment and buying decision is important to the prospect, deciding to buy right away from the first person that shows up to sell him is not on his agenda.

<u>The No B.S. Truth:</u> Only a tiny percentage of the audience you market to will be ready to buy right now from that one single piece of marketing you send out.

As a matter of fact, Chet Holmes (legendary sales & marketing executive who ran 9 divisions for billionaire Charlie Munger's company) found these revealing stats about ANY marketplace:

- Only about <u>5%</u> of the market is ready to buy right now.

- About <u>65%</u> of the market are either: interested **OR** can be made to be interested but just aren't **YET** ready to buy right now.

- Finally, around <u>30%</u> of the market will **NEVER** buy from you no matter what, even if it was free.

These marketplace statistics don't change. You can bet on these numbers being very close to accurate. Given these facts, the question is:

"What do we do with the 65% who are either interested or can be made to be interested in our proposition?"

First, we must get them to raise their hands and identify themselves as "interested" by doing lead generation advertising.

Second, we must invest in **Strategic Repetition.** You must have repetition if you want to maximise the monetary potential of every lead you obtain.

Not One-Shot Marketing where you send out only one promotional piece and hope they'll buy. You MUST have repetition if you want to be effective and profitable in your marketing.

You do this by installing a **MULTI-STEP Campaign to follow up with the leads** you've acquired but have not yet turned into happy paying customers.

This involves sending out a series of relevant communications that take place over a short period of time, each one reiterating your offer and your call to action. They could be letters, emails, texts, postcards or phone calls.

The fastest way to get started with this is to use a **Three-Step Follow-Up Sequence**, often used in the collection industry.

Collection letters work like this: first notice, second notice, third notice—each about 15 days apart. Each letter refers to the previous one they sent. And each gets tougher and tougher until the last letter, rubber stamped "Final Notice."

Think about it: If these collection letters can get money from people who don't have any, offering them nothing... What would happen if we tried the same process on people who DO have money, and offered them SOMETHING they actually want, need or have an interest in.

You can easily apply this to your Lead Conversion System.

Here's what the <u>THREE-STEP follow-up sequence</u> looks like:

1. **Restate, Resell, and Extend the Same Offer:** When someone doesn't buy or take action, it doesn't necessarily mean they don't want what you offer. There are different reasons why people don't respond or buy.

   Your job is to identify these reasons, acknowledge and eliminate them in your follow-up. Answer them as persuasively and honestly as possible. Then restate, resell, and extend the same offer with a new deadline for response.

2. **Provide a Stern or Humorous "Second Notice" Tied to an Impending Deadline:** Choose to be stern or humorous depending on your style and WHO you're talking to.

   If they're suffering from a serious problem with serious consequences, it's probably better if your language is stern. Then, present either the same or a slightly altered offer again, emphasizing the penalty of missing the deadline.

3. **"Third and Final Notice":** You can present the same offer again. But you also have the option to <u>sweeten the offer</u>. Make it a truly irresistible "take it or leave it" final offer.

   Re-emphasize the oncoming deadline, the disappearance of the offer, the pain they'll continue to endure if they don't take action, and why they'll get close to their hearts desire if they do take action on your offer.

<u>Bonus Step #4:</u> **Change the Offer.** Most people give up on their unconverted leads too soon.

Just because your unconverted leads didn't take the next step with your initial offer does not mean their need, interest, or desire for the outcome that your solution provides is gone.

They are simply telling you they don't like your offer right now. But their desire to solve their problem is still there. Their desire for achieving the outcome and transforming their lives is still there. You just have to package the offer <u>differently.</u>

Here are a few simple and fast ways you may want to change your offer: by introducing new bonuses and premiums, new payment terms, giving them extended deadlines, free services, and other new incentives. Brainstorm.

Boost Your Credibility With Additional Content

Having a multi-step campaign already puts you way ahead of most of your competitors who only make one contact with leads or none at all. Even so, **there are times when you need to extend the sales timeline to further boost your authority and credibility.**

You do so by following up on the initial lead generation magnet (LGM) with additional, related content.

For example, you get a new lead who has opted to get your LGM of a video training on a specific topic. In order to establish your authority and credibility with your newly acquired lead, you follow up that initial video training with a series of related content.

You can follow up with a number of content pieces: more video training, emails, reports, guides, checklists, tools, templates, helpful articles, books, online workshops, webinars etc.

Hold off asking for the sale until the very end. Once a lead is captured, you don't have to make an offer right away.

If you wish to establish solid authority positioning in the minds of your prospects first, you can choose to provide additional information relevant to the topic of the LGM that they've initially asked for.

Each new piece of content should end with a "stay tuned for coming attractions" message. You want to keep your leads curious and looking forward to your next message—like the cliffhangers you see on films and TV. This message looks something like this:

"As an added bonus for subscribing, I'm going to be sending you my best *[Insert Additional Content: video training, blog posts, articles, reports, case studies, etc.]*. It's about *[Insert relevant topic related to the LGM]*. Be on the lookout for an email from me tomorrow."

The final piece of content in this follow-up series is where you would make your real call-to-action, laying out all the vital elements of your "Consultation" or "Buy Now" Offer—its features, benefits, price or payment options, guarantee, bonuses, etc.

Show Up Like NO ONE ELSE With: The "Shock and Awe" Package

A Shock and Awe Package is **a physical box you mail to carefully selected, high-probability and most ideal prospects.**

It's filled with high value content designed to overwhelm the prospect with extreme evidence that you are indeed head and shoulders above any other business in your category (or any other option available to them).

The goal of a Shock & Awe Package is to prepare and condition your prospect so that before they even have the first conversation with you, they already view you as a trusted advisor, already understand what to expect and are predisposed to doing business with you—with little to no price or sales resistance.

All this happens BEFORE the sale. It's an essential piece that takes you out of the dog-and-pony show that everybody else is doing to get appointments, and instead, lets your marketing do the heavy lifting for you.

Most of the questions, objections and concerns of your prospects will be handled by your Shock & Awe box.

This means **you no longer have to meet with anyone who is not qualified, conditioned and properly prepared to do business with you, unless and until they've gone through your Shock & Awe package.**

Your Shock & Awe Package could include all sorts of different authority-building, trust-building, and educational components:

- **Cover Letter (also called Lift Letter):** Reminding people why you're sending them this package. In this case, they have requested information on a specific topic of interest.

  Tell them what you've included and why. Tell them how to consume the contents inside and what you want them to do after they've gone through your package.

- **Consumer Report Guides/Special Reports:** Reports and

guides written by you demonstrate and position you as the expert. Don't forget your Call to Action (CTA) at the end telling them what you want them to do next, giving clear instructions.

- **Checklist/Evaluation Questions:** Create a list of questions prospects should use to evaluate their choices and make an intelligent buying decision. Demonstrate the benefits you deliver and your USP.

  Also outline the disadvantages of other options. You want to highlight the cons of using other alternatives whilst also explaining the benefits you uniquely deliver. Use this as a "silent sales tool" that positions you as the unique and only answer to all their questions and concerns.

- **CD/DVDs:** Interviews, guest appearances, podcasts, presentations, case studies, testimonials etc.—anything showcasing your authority and expertise. Put them in there even if your prospects don't have a CD or DVD player.

  You want to create the perception of value and personalisation because something delivered physically almost always has more perceived value than something delivered online. On the CD or DVD, you may even add a note: "to watch this online, go to this website."

- **Testimonials and Reviews:** What others say about you is far more important than what you say about yourself. So include anything and everything positive anyone has ever said about you. Show overwhelming proof (not just 2 or 3) that you are trustworthy, you deliver on your promise, and the only appropriate choice they should go with.

- **Here's What Happens When You Work With Me/Us:** Explain how you serve your customers. Show them what the process looks like when they work with you—in writing or through a visual presentation. People are afraid of uncertainty and the unknown. This piece helps people have clarity in what to expect and feel more comfortable.

- **Entertainment:** Grabbers (items that grab attention) and/or fun things that tie into your message or your business. Send small gifts that make people feel special.

  Don't limit your thinking to only sending out "information." You can include accessories, t-shirts, cookies, anything that you believe might engage your prospect's attention and interest.

- **Book:** If you're the author of a book, you are automatically an authority in the minds of your prospects. Again, think of it as a positioning tool. Author = Authority.

Present Your Consultation Offer

Everything we've covered so far in your Lead Development & Conversion Follow-Up System leads to this one component: **getting the prospect to invite you to a meeting, appointment,**

consultation or sales event.

The power of building this out into a sequential, multi-step process, with your LGM at the beginning, is that it creates a slippery slope where the prospect is saying "YES" through an ongoing course of *micro-agreements.* Think of it like this:

- ✓ The prospect says "YES" to the Lead Generation Ad and Lead Magnet (LGM)…

- ✓ Then says "YES" to opening a follow-up email regarding the topic of your LGM…

- ✓ Then says "YES" to getting your additional content or shock & awe package…

- ✓ Then says "YES" to watching your online video training series…

- ✓ Then says "YES" to reading your book or special report… so on and so forth

Until he finally says "YES" to seeking you out for your expertise and asking you for a consultation. When he comes to you for his first consultation, how do you think he'll perceive you?

Will he see you as "just another salesman"? Or do you think he'll come in with the confidence he's seeing a trusted advisor who can finally put an end to all his worries and frustrations?

How difficult do you think he will be if he comes in already believing that you're the one who can solve his problem?

This is a powerful environment to be selling in because it creates a *Commitment to Consistency*, as Robert Cialdini talks about in his best-selling book *Influence*.

We humans have a desire to be (and appear to be) consistent with what we have already done. Thus, once we have made a choice or taken a stand, we are more likely to behave consistently with that commitment.

To set the stage for that "yes consistency", you've got to **get prospects to make that first small/low-risk commitment.** It's this connection between commitment and consistency that makes it easier for somebody to say "yes" and to keep doing so.

That low-risk commitment often starts by offering a free or very low-priced yet high value Lead Generation Magnet. When marketing and selling your high-ticket goods and services that often requires a longer sales process, the premise is simple:

Obtain a large purchase by starting with a small one. Any small, low-risk sale will do. The purpose of this sale is not profit. It is commitment.

This is why we want to **start our marketing system with lead generation advertising, offering our low-risk (typically free) LGM, then work our way towards a consultation offer by getting the prospect to say "yes" to a series of micro-commitments.** Read that again. It cost me a small fortune and years and years of trial-and-error to figure this out.

If you look at most small business owners who sell medium to high-ticket products or services, you'll notice they often do the opposite, which is obviously a very costly mistake.

They're all trying to sell directly and overtly and asking the prospect to make a very big commitment on the very first encounter. Sure, they'll get some sales, but at what cost?

At the cost of an enormous amount of time and money being wasted on trying to sell to badly conditioned and badly prepared prospects who don't end up being good customers in the long run.

That's why it's a better long-term strategy to start off with a low risk offer and then do follow-up marketing to get the prospect to say "yes" to a series of micro-commitments.

Important: If the deal does not close, do NOT give up. Too many opportunities are lost just because the prospect (assuming they were carefully selected and properly prepared) said "no" in the first meeting.

In other words, they said yes to the appointment; they attended the appointment; but they didn't buy. In this situation, you must deploy an **"Appointment—No Sale" Follow-Up Campaign.**

It consists of the same components we have talked about here. Continue to send out a series of relevant communications and components of the Lead Development & Conversion System you deem necessary.

This can include more content, more Shock and Awe, more

multi-step campaigns of email, direct mail, phone calls, postcards, text, etc., and more irresistible offers (with compelling bonuses, guarantees, payment options and other incentives to "sweeten the pot").

Do not give up. There's a whole bunch of reasons why the prospect might say no. The important thing to know is that the prospect's desire to gain an advantage or avoid pain is still there, waiting to be satisfied.

You've already done all this work. It'll be a shame if you let your competitors swoop in now to snatch the sale away from you.

One month, three months or six months down the line, your prospect may be ready again and when they are, you will be top of mind as The trusted advisor they will actively seek.

"How Often Do I Show Up?"

The most important thing to know is **there is no such thing as showing up too often to someone who has expressed interest in the topic you're showing up about. Relevance gets you welcome. Irrelevance gets you unsubscribers.**

If somebody has clearly expressed to you that they have a problem, an unmet need, or a strong desire about something, then they have invited an almost unlimited amount of follow-up from you as long as it's relevant to their problems and desires.

Of course, if they no longer want to hear from you, make sure you always give them the option to opt-out or unsubscribe. Don't worry about the unsubscribers. Chances are, most of them weren't genuine prospects in the first place. Just tire-kickers and people looking to get something for nothing.

The serious prospects won't unsubscribe. They're always waiting for just the right spark that'll get them to act on their heart's desires.

So show up as often as you can with something relevant to their problem and try to move the ball forward if they want to solve that problem, starting with small micro-commitments by presenting low risk offers, then a consultation, ultimately leading to the sale.

Final Words About Your Lead Development & Conversion System

Once this system has been built, it doesn't need to be rebuilt. You may change, restructure, or repurpose certain component pieces according to relevance and market factors, but you do not have to start from scratch and rebuild them again.

While it does initially require you to invest time, money and effort to create the marketing assets and materials, once it's working, it will keep on working like a well-oiled machine.

All you would need to do is to maintain the system. This consists of monitoring, checking and updating things accordingly, making sure nothing breaks.

Chapter 12: How to Get Booked Solid and Dominate Your Local "Target Market" in 45 Days or Less—Even During Times Of Uncertainty

Truth be told, **most of the overt and proactive marketing & advertising done by small businesses to get new customers, clients or patients are horribly unsuccessful.**

I critique hundreds of promotional pieces all the time and quite frankly, **most small business advertising and marketing today just flat-out STINKS!**

Everybody is just blindly copying their competitors or big dumb companies without any real thought or strategy behind what they're doing and why they're doing it.

When everybody looks and sounds the same, nobody stands out, and the prospect is left with more confusion, overwhelm and frustration.

There is great power in standing out from the crowd. That means great power is bound for the business or person that defies all the norms and goes the opposite direction to everyone else.

For your business to truly thrive in 2024 and beyond, you must **become and be seen as The expert in your category.**

When a consumer cannot find an expert he can trust, he seeks a vendor with only one thing in mind: Lowest price. Foolishly fighting this battle is a sure path to failure and bankruptcy.

A true expert doesn't need to overtly advertise his core goods or services like everybody else.

Instead, a true expert first **POSITIONS** himself as an expert (not as a vendor or salesperson), then engineers a process where he is simply sought after by his ideal prospects who are serious and eager to receive his help.

Make no mistake, this doesn't just happen by random chance or luck. The process of having new customers coming to you, almost begging to do business with you happens through **deliberate intent** and **application.**

The good news is, there's a very certain way to getting booked solid as a small business or service provider and stay that way for years without ever having to be pushy or overtly "sell" your products or services...

AND without bashing people over the heads with massive discounts that eat at your profit margins, or wasting time having to chase "would be" and "could be" buyers.

If you're a serious business owner, the good news is that even after I describe it to hundreds of business owners, hardly any will actually take action on it... for a variety of reasons.

Laziness, low self-esteem, self-limiting beliefs, fear of criticism, poor understanding of how money works and thus being a cheapskate etc. Whatever the reason for non-action is, it is hardly ever because of actual lack of money or resources or ideas.

Further, **a big problem for most people in any business niche or category is they only hang out with their own kind.**

They put their wagons in a circle and look at each other, copying each other (trying to only do a little bit better), and ignoring everyone and everything outside that circle. Remember, when everybody is saying and doing the same thing, nobody stands out.

With those cautions, I will now introduce you to a radically different approach to dominating your local "target market" in 45 days or less, even in times of uncertainty.

Regrettably, this is so foreign to most business owners' thinking, it may take a while for you to really "get it." Let us hope you are exceptional, because I'm going to sketch it out for you here in very abbreviated form.

Step #1: Big Fish, Small Pond

As I described in Chapter 6, **most business owners, service providers, and sales professionals are playing Blind Archery.**

They have been taught and led to believe that their "target market" is anyone and everyone with a wallet and a pulse. This leads to a lot of waste in money, time and resources.

The old theory is that if you broadcast your message enough times in every direction, you are bound to win an audience. This is no different from the frustrated sales guy who cold calls a thousand prospects in the hopes that ten will agree to an appointment and then one will *hopefully* buy.

As I've said over and over again, only a tiny percentage of any market are actually ready to buy right now, and an even smaller percentage are ready to buy from you.

We can do better. Instead, **when resources are limited, what we must decide to do is become a "Big Fish In A Small Pond."** You want to target a specific market with a specific problem. Small enough that the resources you're willing to commit give you tremendous impact.

To define your "small pond", ask yourself these questions:

1. **Who?** — Who is the specific customer, client or patient you are trying to reach? Get to know them, define them, and

understand their behaviours and motivations. The better we can define our exact "Who", the better our chances of crafting a Message that will truly resonate with them. You can narrow down your target market via Geographic, Demographic and Psychographic factors, as discussed in Chapter 6.

2. **Why?** — Why is this important? Why are you doing this? Why do you serve your dream customer, client or patient? You must have a good "reason why" for showing up to the marketplace. Most people don't have one. They just show up with huge discounts whenever they feel desperate to get customers in the door.

3. **Need/Benefits?** — What needs are you fulfilling? What does that preferred prospect want from you, and what problem will be solved? Why haven't these problems and frustrations been solved? Have they been let down in the past by previous vendors—if so, what makes you different?

Who are your "best" customers? Look back and think about who you really like working with, and if possible, would love to clone and multiply. What type of person are you really for? What specific problem are you really trying to solve?

This **narrowly defined segment of your market** is your "Small Pond." You decide what that small pond is for your business.

Instead of wasting time and money trying to market and sell to mostly unqualified prospects, you can narrow down your target audience to your "Small Pond" and focus most of your time, money and resources on them.

Focusing your resources on your Small Pond will sharpen your message and you'll have more money to spend than your competitors who are all burning cash by targeting anybody and everybody with a wallet and a pulse.

The "big fish, small pond" approach is best for anybody operating with limited resources, and who isn't?

When somebody describes their market too broadly, I know they are doomed to failure, if for no other reason than the disparity between their limited resources and what it will take to have any impact on that big and broad of a market.

Step #2: Create An Irresistible Offer Exclusively FOR Your Ideal Customer, Client or Patient

You need an **Irresistible Offer—a "widget" to sell specifically created for your narrowly defined target market (your Small Pond).**

Your offer needs to be able to communicate to your market "If you're an X type of person suffering from Y problem, and you want Z transformation, then this offer is <u>specifically for you</u>."

For instructions on creating Irresistible Offers and to see an example you can model, go back to Chapter 7. Go back to the Bob Stupak example, study it, and model it for your purposes.

Now, it's important to understand that your offer could still be a bundle of similar goods or services you offer to the general public (with a few relevant tweaks to fit your specific market). That's absolutely fine.

What matters is you **effectively communicate** (in your Marketing message) to your ideal prospects that you created this offer to solve a specific, nagging problem in their lives that they feel is **unique to** *them.*

Remember, it's all about them and what they want. It's about their problems, pains, worries, frustrations, wants, desires, hopes and dreams.

You are not merely selling a product or service. No. You are selling a **transformation.** How will it *transform* their lives for the better? You are also selling **meaning.** What will acting on your offer and reaping its benefits *mean* to them?

Again, in order to come up with a truly irresistible offer, you've got to understand your WHO. You've really got to know their mental and emotional state when they first find you. It was the legendary marketer and copywriter, Robert Collier, who said:

"Enter the conversation already happening in your prospect's mind."

This is one of the most important marketing principles. Most businesses don't enter the conversation in the prospect's mind.

Instead, they enter it by shoving their products and services down the prospect's throat. Hence why most marketing & advertising fails.

So for the most part, if you're targeting a cold audience, don't start your message with the product, service, or whatever you're selling. That's not the conversation going on in their minds. Again, this highlights the importance of knowing your customer.

In order to craft a truly compelling message that "enters the conversion already happening in their minds", you must find out what they REALLY want from the solution you provide.

For instance, you'll see **financial planners** competing with one another offering "estate plans" to 55+ year olds. Not that there's anything wrong with offering estate planning.

However, the message can be rephrased with something that's more relevant to the conversation currently going on in their prospects' minds.

Compare the phrasing "Looking for an estate plan?" to… *"Interested in a solution to take care of your family when you're gone?*

Now that's a much stronger, more emotional way of connecting with the prospect. It uses terms and phrasing that resonates with the topic currently going on in their heads, constantly worrying them and keeping them up at night.

Another example: If you are in **Sales**—a broad industry but for the sake of convenience, let's say it's any business that requires you to sell via person-to-person call or meeting.

Salespeople are just like marketers in the sense that they love to talk more about themselves and how great their products or services are rather than investing time to truly understand what the prospect is looking for and cares about.

You've probably encountered plenty of salespeople who made you feel like they were only talking to you for the commission.

The most successful salespeople I've seen are usually **the ones who put extra time and effort into the relationship first,** before ever talking about how great they are.

The winners are the ones who put in the time to really understand your problem and prescribe a customised solution based on the information you give them.

What does that tell us about what people really want from a sales professional? **They want to FEEL IMPORTANT.**

They often don't want to hear about how great you are without first feeling like you really care about helping them solve their problem and reach their desired goals. Stephen Covey wisely said in his book *The 7 Habits of Highly Effective People*: ***"Seek First To Understand, Then To Be Understood."***

Last example: if you were a **service-based business**, why should they choose your service over every other service provider out there?

This will vary depending on the service you provide but a lot of this comes down to showing people that you are an expert in your field; showing people that you care about their needs more than yours and by consistently providing excellent service where they feel like they can trust you to help them make the right decisions and not mess things up.

In short, **people want you to show them that they can count on you and reassure them that you'll take good care of them.**

It's important to really understand your market and their unspoken needs and desires before you even spend any time creating an offer.

Because HOW you communicate your offer is often more important than the features or deliverables of the offer itself. This formula may sound extremely simplistic, but it's true: *Figure out what people really want and offer it to them.*

You can often take your generic offer and make it irresistible to a specific market simply by <u>wrapping</u> it in their problems, wants and desires—and giving the offer a unique, relevant and attention-grabbing name.

So while your goods or services remain the same, the way it's positioned, communicated and promoted is totally different and specific for that narrow target market only (your Small Pond).

Why? Because although the deliverables are the same, the MEANING is different. People attach different values and meanings towards different things.

The Secret to Getting Infinitely Higher Response: **Each one of us sincerely believes that ourselves, our situation, and our needs are unique and different.**

We are therefore most responsive to someone who acknowledges that "feeling of uniqueness" and is somehow well-matched or expert in our unique scenario.

That's the key to crafting truly irresistible marketing messages and offers. Specifically match your Offer (and overall Message) to the problems, pains and desires of your specific Market.

Don't forget to effectively communicate the benefits of your offer. Don't just give them a list of features.

Most of the time, your market does not know what these features mean. But what they DO understand are the benefits they'll reap for taking you up on your offer. So speak their language.

The easiest, fastest, most effective way to do this is to **build a list of Offer Features and Benefits.**

List every possible feature and benefit of your offer, then organise them by importance. Very simple, yet most will still choose to be lazy about this and refuse.

Step #3: Lead Generation Advertising To Get "Raised Hands"

Once you've worked out the features and benefits of your irresistible offer, the next thing you need is a **Lead Generation AD** and a **Lead Generation MAGNET (LGM).**

If you're not sure what lead generation is, why it's important, and how to do it properly, go back to Chapter 10 for the full masterclass on it.

Now that we've got our Irresistible Offer specifically matched to our carefully selected narrow market, we now need to write our Lead Generation Ad offering our LGM.

Such an ad DOES NOT advertise your goods or services. The purpose of a lead generation ad is to advertise your LGM: a book, special report, consumer's guide, checklist, templates, a webinar or masterclass, a quiz, an in-person workshop or seminar, etc.

You can choose to use a range of appropriate media channels to deliver your message, but for this example, let's just say **you're using simple, dirt-cheap postcards.** You'll mail these postcards to a list of your highest-probability prospects.

For example, we're sending postcards via direct mail to 5,000 homes of men aged 45 to 55, who live in specific (more affluent) postcodes in South West England, married with two or more children, a homeowner, and have an estimated household income of £120,000 per year.

Yes, with direct mail, you can get THAT specific.

It starts with knowing your WHO. Once you know who your ideal prospects are, you can buy or rent a mailing list that closely matches their geographic and demographic information from mailing list vendors like:

- www.selectabase.co.uk for UK mailing lists… or

- https://lists.nextmark.com for US mailing lists

This means you're not starting from the big, broad, unwashed masses. You're eliminating a lot of waste in advertising and saving thousands of pounds because <u>you're already starting with very sophisticated, precise target marketing</u>.

You're filtering out the majority of the non-prospects and only speaking to the best potential prospects that fit your criteria.

Here's a **done-for-you postcard template** that I've written so you don't have to do it yourself.

Feel free to use it and profit from it. Tweak it for your specific business and purposes (can also be adapted for online ads):

Front of Postcard:

Would You Like to [Solve Biggest Problem] So YOU Can

Experience [Desired End Result/Outcome]?

Free Report Reveals "Title of Your Report"

Go to: www.YourURL.com or call xxxxx-xxx-xxx

Back of Postcard:

ATTENTION [Target Prospect]: FREE Consumer Report
Guide Reveals...

How to [Solve Biggest Problem] So YOU Can Experience

[Desired End Result/Outcome] — GUARANTEED!

Dear Friend,

If you're ready to finally [Solve Biggest Problem], then I have
some very good news...

My FREE Consumer Report Guide — [Lead Magnet Title] —
reveals exactly how you can experience [Desired End
Result/Outcome] and overcome the challenges of [Problem #1],
[Problem #2], and even [Problem #3].

Best of all, I'm going to send everything to you 100% FREE — just
call us at [Insert Phone Number] or go to www.YourURL.com
and we'll mail it out to you immediately! (You don't even have to
pay for postage).

The ad then directs them to a Squeeze Page (also known as a "Lead Capture Page") where they can give their contact information in exchange for your Lead Generation Magnet (LGM), which in this case, is your free report.

By the way, I know I've given a simple postcard example but remember, the media is just the vehicle you use to deliver your message to the right prospects.

If your ideal prospects hang out online, on Facebook for example, you can take this exact "Lead Generation" process and tweak it to fit that media platform.

Anyway, I'm not going to write the entire lead generation and marketing campaign here for you. I get paid a ton of dough to do that. But ultimately, the ad offers a free report (or any other type of LGM you deem appropriate) that reveals genuine valuable information about the problem they're having.

It helps them make an informed decision on what they can and should do next. Obviously, one of those solutions would be to come to you—either to buy now or schedule an appointment.

The most important part of your lead generation campaign is the fact that **you now have a bank of qualified leads whom you can continue to follow up with and present offers to.**

You no longer have to pay to get these prospects to step out of the crowd and identify themselves. You can now actually invest more money in marketing to them because you know they've expressed interest in your particular solution.

In other words, you're talking to people who have "raised their hands" and invited you in for further communication on the topic. So you're not an annoying pest, you're a welcome guest.

Step #4: A "Really Good" Sales Letter Selling Your Irresistible Offer

By now, you should have a bank of good quality leads who have stepped forward and identified themselves as having interest in what you sell.

Next, we need to **turn those leads into booked appointments and/or paying customers, clients or patients.**

We do that by sending these leads a really good sales letter selling them your Irresistible Offer—the offer you specifically made to help solve their problem. The format of this sales letter can either be video (video sales letter/VSL) or simply text.

Often, the most obvious "next step" call to action is to invite them to come in for a consultation or to buy now. Here's a solid **formula for writing a high-converting sales letter:**

1. Pre-Head that identifies (or calls out) WHO the Offer is for

2. Attention-Getting Headline that makes the single, BIGGEST Promise

3. Subheadline that explains or expands on the promise

4. State the Problem

5. Agitate the Problem

6. Solve the Problem / Present your Solution

7. Describe the Offer in detail: Offer name/title, Bullets of Features and Benefits, Present Bonuses, Answer Objections, State Price, Give Guarantee, Set Deadline

8. Final Call-to-Action (CTA) with clear instructions on what they should do next

9. P.S. — Reiterate why they need to act NOW and the penalty/pain for inaction or delay

Regarding numbers 4, 5, and 6: It's a powerful *copywriting formula* known as **P-A-S: Problem, Agitate, Solve.**

It works based on the premise that **people are more likely to take action in order to move away from pain than they are to move towards pleasure or gain.** It may be the most reliable sales formula ever invented.

In psychology, this is associated with the theory of Loss Aversion which states that the pain of loss is twice as powerful as the pleasure of gain.

As a result, we are more likely to avoid pain in whatever way possible. This is why understanding the problems and frustrations of your WHO is so important.

<u>Here's how the P-A-S formula works.</u>

Step one is to define the prospect's Problem. Acknowledge the problem in the way your prospect would describe it in his/her own thoughts. Sometimes, the problem is something they can't even verbalise yet, but they know they're experiencing pain because of it.

It matters very little whether you're addressing a problem they know they have or don't yet know they have. Either way, the prospect is feeling pain, so say only enough to acknowledge that pain and relate it in his own words to get him in agreement.

Step two is Agitation. Once the problem is established clearly and factually, it's time to inject emotion. We expand on the pains and frustrations the prospect is experiencing because of the problem. In doing so, we stir up his emotional responses.

We tap into his anger, resentment, guilt, embarrassment, fear— any and every applicable negative emotion. We want to make the problem larger than life, worse than death.

The third and final step is to present the Solution. You've now stated the problem. You've created tremendous agitation about the problem and caused your readers to stand up, shaking their heads and pacing the room, muttering "This has got to stop! What can I do about this? Who can help me with this?" It's at this point that you introduce the solution—YOUR solution.

Now you have the perfect opportunity to talk about your goods, services, offers and the accompanying benefits. Notice how vastly different and superior this approach is compared to how most people do it.

Rather than taking up lots of space and beginning your message with "me, me, me" talk, you start your message with your prospect. You're making it about them.

Once your prospect realises that you understand his worries and frustrations, he will want to hear about a solution; this is your invitation to start talking about yourself and what you provide.

Make sure you have at least one Call-To-Action (CTA) at the end of every ad, sales letter, sales page, email etc., with specific, clear instructions on what to do next.

Don't leave it up to them to do guesswork. Tell them exactly what to do, how to do it, and what to expect. For best chances of success, you want to sprinkle **multiple** CTAs all throughout your ad, email, sales letter etc.

*Copywriting is one-half of what I do. The other is strategic marketing & consulting. If you'd like a "copywriting critique" on your current ads, sales letters, emails, website content, brochures, etc., you are entitled to redeem one free "2nd Opinion" Critique Certificates (which I typically charge $250.00/£200.00 for) that you get as a FREE bonus gift with this book.

Step 5: Booked Solid, Famous, and The Dominant Force in Your Local "Target Market" in 45 Days or Less

Let's talk numbers. Let's say that you sent your lead generation postcards to a targeted mailing list of 5,000 of your ideal customers.

For simplicity, say that a mere 5% of those people respond to get your free report, or any other LGM you're offering.

As an aside, you'll probably get less than 5% response rate if you're targeting a broader market, but if you're very selective in your targeting process, and you have a carefully chosen your "Small Pond," you'll be able resonate more with your prospects and so a 5% response rate is very much possible.

Anyway, that gives you 250 high quality leads who have stepped out of the crowd and identified themselves as "interested" in what you have to say.

This allows you to follow up with them with additional content to boost your authority and credibility. Ultimately, you'll want to sell them something and move them on to the next step, so you'll send your sales letter to them.

So for example, fifteen days later, you send your "really good sales letter" to those 250 leads. You get a modest 10% response from people who, depending on what you're selling, either booked an appointment or have made a first-time purchase.

Now you have 25 first-time buyers in the door... or at least prospects who are very eager to buy and therefore want to have a conversation with you via an appointment.

Remember that because you've taken the time and effort to show them you understand their situation and what they really want, you've developed trust and they're coming to you predetermined to do business with you and now perceive you as an expert authority in your field.

Now, let's say that instead of sending only one really good sales letter to your leads, you send THREE really good sales letters using the **Three-Step Follow-Up Sequence** we talked about in Chapter 11, each letter sent 15 days apart.

From the 250 leads you acquired, another 10% are converted from "merely interested" leads to booked appointments or first-time buyers. That's **a total of 50 highly qualified prospects or new customers in the door.**

And IF you know what you're doing to further monetize and maximise the profitability of each new-customer relationship, then there's a good chance they'll refer at least one of their friends and family to you.

Provided that you delivered (and continue to deliver) excellent service or product, there's a real good chance they will.

That makes **a total of ONE HUNDRED highly qualified**

prospects or new customers in the door. To put it in context, that's 100 of your most ideal prospects coming to you, begging to do business with you, if they can and if you'll let them.

Keep in mind that these are very modest, conservative numbers. You started with a targeted list of only 5,000 people.

If you only increased your geographic range allowing you to target 10,000 ideal prospects, then you can expect to have at least 200 of your dream customers, clients or patients beating a path to your door—all from a simple 45-day campaign.

At this point, it doesn't even matter what the "cost" of the mailing is because there is none. Here's what I mean.

For the sake of convenience, let's say you sell a £1,000 product or service. It costs you £100 to get one good quality lead. So your Cost Per Lead is £100. For every 5 new leads, at least one turns into a new customer, client or patient. So your Cost Per Sale/New Customer is £500.

Now say for five straight years, (or however long your average customer relationship is), the average new customer gives you another £1,000, twice a year. That makes your average Customer Lifetime Value £10,000. *(Math: £2,000 x 5 years)*

Knowing these numbers, if you really wanted to, you COULD spend £10,000 to acquire one good customer. You can afford to do so because that's how much each one is worth to you over the course of your business relationship (in this example, 5 years).

Of course, in reality, it may not be feasible to be working on a loss for five straight years trying to break even.

<u>Still, don't miss the point:</u> **Most business owners are WAY too cheap about investing time, money and resources to get good quality leads and buyers.**

If you have a robust marketing system & strategy in place, if you know your numbers, and if you know how much the average customer is worth over their entire business relationship with you, then you know that the return FAR outweighs the cost.

This is how money is made in marketing. This is how you win at this game. It's not about being cheap trying to lower the cost of acquiring leads and buyers. That's how dumb businesspeople and marketers do it.

Smart businesspeople who succeed in today's economy don't care about lowest cost per lead or customer. They care about **being able to spend MORE** in order to get a good lead and buyer.

They care about ROI over the period of the entire business relationship. So once you get a new customer, client or patient, the game now becomes about getting them to buy more, stay for longer, and refer others to you.

A Personal Message From The Author + Your FREE GIFTS

Dear Reader,

This can be the beginning or the end.

I know this book hasn't been light reading.

If you're just starting out in business or new to marketing, some of the ideas, strategies and concepts I talk about here can be overwhelming.

If you're a seasoned vet, this book has probably further clarified and validated some of your pre-existing beliefs about marketing and the business you're really in.

Regardless, I hope I have given you actionable and eye-opening insights about marketing, advertising and business in general.

Now that you've finished the book, you're probably asking

yourself **"What should I do next?"**

Whether you're a seasoned pro or just starting out, you probably bought this book looking for a positive change in your business and in your personal life.

Well, there are three simple steps to positive change:

1. **AWARENESS** of the Problem

2. **DECISION** To Succeed

3. Massive, Deliberate, and Consistent **ACTION**

With this book, you have in your hands, **Awareness.** Awareness of the fact that you need to engineer a system to attract only the best-qualified prospects and eliminate all the waste in your marketing and advertising.

You know that you don't have to rely on "throwing mud against the wall hoping it sticks" type of marketing or be dependent on vendors, agencies or "wizards."

You are aware that to be successful in business today, you must separate yourself from the competition and take the road less travelled.

You realise that you must construct an **organised system** by which you can consistently, predictably and profitably get more leads, customers, clients or patients (rather than doing random and erratic acts of attempted marketing).

Now you've come to the end of the book. You face a **Decision** that has the potential to transform and reinvent your business.

The legendary attorney Gerry Spence almost always closed his ending speech to juries by telling an old parable about a wise old man and a smart-aleck boy. I'll tell it here because I think it has an important message for achieving the life you want as a person and as a business owner.

So every Saturday, the wise elder made himself available for the villagers to line up and ask for his advice. The smart-aleck boy was envious of this and so he devised a plan to humiliate and expose the wise old man as a fool.

He went out into the wilderness and captured a small bird. With the bird cupped to his hands, his plan was to go up to the old man and say "Old man, is the bird alive? Or is it dead?"

If the old man said the bird is "dead," the boy would open his hands and let the bird fly off free.

But if the old man said the bird is "alive," then the boy would crush it; crush it until all the life was out of the bird and it was dead. But the old man proved truly wise, and said...

"The bird is in your hands, my son."

And so, friend, you have a **Decision** to make.

One, nod in agreement, laugh or daydream about doing all these things, transforming your marketing and business life altogether, only to then talk yourself out of it and decide to continue doing what you've normally been doing anyway. Thus, continue getting little to no results, endlessly struggling to make ends meet—just like most business owners today.

Or two, take the road less travelled and decide to take deliberate action on what you've learned today. Like most people who are excellent at their craft, you probably know you're better than most in your field, yet you're not seeing the same success as other lesser competitors. Today could be the day you change that.

It was Mark Twain who said, "The man who does not read has no advantage over the man who cannot read."

It's tough to out-quote Mark Twain, but Johann Wolfgang von Goethe may have when he said, ***"To know and not do, is not to know."***

Every entrepreneurial achievement begins with a Decision. One of the most important is the decision to take **Action.**

Business today is overly complicated, noisy, frustrating, overwhelming and can feel very lonely. One of my early mentors, Bill Glazer, once said that Entrepreneurship is the loneliest pursuit.

Let's not make this the end of a book—read, shelved and never to be seen again. Let's make this the **beginning** of an exciting, ongoing and profitable relationship.

As a reader of this book, I would like to invite you to:

Join The FREE 5-Day Magnetic Marketing Challenge: How To Go From 'Annoying Pest' To A 'Welcome Guest' <u>Using MY Special Link</u>

I'll also give you a <u>**$696.95 BRIBE**</u> just for joining. Here are my personal gifts to you when you join using my special link:

Personal Gift #1: The "Automatic Appointments" System & Toolkit ($397.00 Value)

Whether you're just starting out or have been in business for a few years, you've probably been wanting to create compelling marketing & advertising content…

But like most small business owners, you're starting out from a very limited budget and resources, and you don't want to risk spending thousands per month on hit-or-miss marketing agencies, copywriters, or AI robots…

All that ends today.

The "Automatic Appointments" System & Toolkit is a complete "done-for-you" kit that covers everything you'll ever need to generate all the leads, appointments and sales that you can possibly handle… **without hiring outside help.**

With this Toolkit, you have the power to create a reliable marketing system that attracts "properly prepared" prospects who are ready, willing, and able to move forward with you...

So you don't have to waste your time creating content from scratch only to end up dealing with tire kickers, price shoppers, bargain hunters and "looky-loos".

That's right. **You never have to start from scratch** because all the marketing & advertising content you'll ever need is 80-90% DONE FOR YOU.

Here's what you'll get:

- Facebook™ Ad Templates *($197.00 value)*

- Lead-Generating "Squeeze Page" Templates *($197.00 value)*

- Sales Letter Template to Convert "Ready To Buy Now" Prospects Into Customers *($497.00 value)*

- 4-Step Email Follow-Up Sequence That Turns "On The Fence" Leads Into Buyers *($197.00 value)*

- "Book-a-Call" Sales Letter Template Within Thank-You Page *($497.00 value)*

- Rapid Long-Form Sales Letter Template That Sells Anything *($497.00 value)*

- Lost Customer Reactivation Email Sequence *($197.00 value)*

- "Stick Letter" Template for Reducing Refunds & Buyer's Remorse *($97.00 value)*

- 4-Step Appointment Reminder Templates For Reducing No-Shows *($97.00 value)*

- Cancellation Policy Templates For Reducing No-Shows & Last-Minute Cancellations *($97.00 value)*

- 5-Step "Cash Flow Surge" Email Sequence *($297.00 value)*

TOTAL VALUE If You Paid For Each Template Separately: $2,670.00

Today, you have a chance to get it all for free and get instant access to it so you can implement and start seeing results right away.

You Can Integrate These Templates Into Your Marketing & Advertising In… **Just 3 Easy Steps:**

1. Instantly download "The Automatic Appointments Toolkit" to your computer

2. Enter a few details about your offer, product, service or business

3. Start getting more (and better) leads, appointments, and sales… without hiring expensive marketing/ad agencies and copywriters

The templates and guidance you'll receive could save you lots of money and years of painful trial and error.

That's why I call it **The ULTIMATE SHORTCUT** for any business wanting to grow but have limited resources… and it can all be yours for FREE. Just make sure you don't forget to send me your success stories once you start getting incredible results.

I hope you not only profit from it, but also enjoy reading the unique content that you create for yourself using this toolkit.

Personal Gift #2: Ultimate Small Business Marketing Plan Template ($49.95 Value)

What is the point of all the tools and templates and spending money on ads and marketing IF you don't have a clear, step-by-step Marketing Plan?

It's like trying to drive in the mountains on a stormy night with broken headlights… Do you know where you're going? Which pitfalls to avoid?

The worst thing you can do for your business is to try and captain it without a clear map and navigational equipment to determine and direct your ship's movements.

Better to avoid the Iceberg now than later. Later is too late.

My "Ultimate Small Business Marketing Plan Template" will help you avoid the icebergs and pitfalls so you can steer your business in the right direction without all the shiny objects and distractions stealing all your time and attention.

This Marketing Plan Template will help you:

- Carefully define, select and really understand your best and highest probability **Target Market**

- Craft compelling **Marketing Messages** that practically forces your audience to stop what they're doing and pay attention

- **Find your USP (Unique Selling Proposition)** so you can separate yourself from the "me too" crowd and get noticed by your ideal prospects

- Choose the perfect **Lead Generation Magnet** that attracts the type of customers, clients or patients who are actually interested in what you're selling

- Quickly build compelling and **Irresistible Offers** that makes it a "no brainer" decision for serious buyers to pull out their wallets and buy

- **Eliminate all the risks of doing business with you…** things that are stopping your prospects from moving forward with you

- Write **attention-grabbing Headlines** with my proven "fill-in-the-blanks" templates—no more writer's block!

The best part is you'll finally have a clear roadmap to help you make the right marketing and advertising decisions for your business —and avoid random and erratic acts of marketing based on other people's opinions.

Personal Gift #3: Hands-On Personal Assistance: "2nd Opinion" Ad Critique ($250.00 Value)

You're entitled to a **FREE "2nd Opinion" Ad Critique**—send any promotional item to me for <u>my personal feedback:</u> any ad, sales letter/page, email, SMS text, landing page etc.

You'll get a report with my honest advice on what you've done well, what you haven't, and how to improve it. (A warning: I go to great lengths to safeguard my time so I'm rather blunt. I may hurt your feelings, but I WILL improve what you're doing!)

As a consultant, I provide this 2nd Opinion Critique Service to business owners, entrepreneurs and sales professionals, and charge $250.00 (or £200.00) per critique. So this IS a very real $250.00 value.

However, it can certainly be worth a whole lot more to you. Advertising legend, John Caples (who made millions of dollars for some of the largest companies in the US before the internet), famously said:

"I have seen one advertisement sell 19.5 TIMES as much goods as another. Both ads occupied the same space. Both were run in the same publication. Both had photos and carefully written copy. The difference was that one used **the right appeal** and the other used **the wrong appeal.**"

In other words, you don't have to wait until you know everything to start seeing results and making money. You can immediately "make your ads pay" TODAY simply by claiming your free 2nd Opinion Ad Critique.

I'll send all these money-making gifts to you absolutely FREE... with ONE CAVEAT:

The ONLY way you can get your hands on my PERSONAL GIFTS is to…

Join The FREE 5-Day Magnetic Marketing Challenge: How To Go From 'Annoying Pest' To A 'Welcome Guest' <u>Using MY Special Link</u>

"What is this and what can I expect from it?", I hear you say.

When you say "yes" and join the challenge for free, my peers and mentors will show you, in just 90-minutes a day for 5 days, how to quickly go from an "annoying pest" to a "welcome guest" in the eyes of your dream customers, clients or patients.

<u>**In this challenge, you'll discover:**</u>

- Why **"magnetically attracting"** can help produce better customers, clients or patients who are happy to pay higher prices!

- How to **transform your customers' WANTS into NEEDS**... and how to position yourself to be their #1 hero they've been searching for…

- **How to craft your winning message** that <u>practically</u> <u>hypnotises customers into buying from you</u>!

- **Why "messaging" is the #1 MOST critical component** of any offer... and how to know if your message is the RIGHT one to use

- **How to form your USP** (Unique Selling Proposition) that'll have you stand-out amongst your competitors as the BEST and ONLY option!

- The **3-step letter sequencing** that pulls in your ideal customer, client, or patient without having to think nearly as hard as you used to

- **Discover the right MEDIA that best fits your target audience** (Is it Facebook or Instagram? What about native or YouTube? Understanding where your audience "hangs out" is a game-changer for any business)

- Why you should **STOP running your business the way MOST business owners "think"** they should be running their business (...this "leap" can shift your business from "cash-strapped" to "cash flow" overnight!)

- **Why NOW more than ever is the perfect time** to apply "magnetic marketing" (especially with rising costs)... to attract clients, customers, and patients without breaking the bank!

And much, MUCH more!

Here's How To Claim Your Free Gifts Today

To take advantage of this offer and get instant access to these money-making resources, simply visit:

www.ArielAstro.co.uk/Gift

Once you're registered, take a screenshot or photo of the "Thank You" page and email it back to Kris at Kris@ArielAstro.co.uk and she'll send you my amazing bonus gifts for free. That's it. Takes less than 2 minutes.

Please note that this offer IS subject to change without notice.

If you're serious about taking your business to the next level—attract rather than chase, get noticed and stand out from the crowd—this is the ideal next step.

I urge you to act on this opportunity today, right now, while it is fresh in your mind.

To Your Success,

Ariel Astrologia

P.S. If you want a more personalised approach; maybe you cannot wait to launch your next campaign…or perhaps want in-depth help in creating your own marketing plan and system… and you want to skip all the trials and tribulations… then schedule permitting, I am available for one-on-one consulting.

P.P.S. If you're not yet ready to have a conversation, as the owner of this book, you are entitled to a FREE "2nd Opinion" Ad Critique. Send any promotional material in for my personal feedback and recommendations. This is a complementary service to help you get results fast, eliminate all the waste in your advertising and increase your flow of leads and buyers.

*Offer subject to change without notice.